Study Guide to Accompany

MONEY, BANKING, AND THE ECONOMY
Sixth Edition

Study Guide to Accompany

MONEY, BANKING, AND THE ECONOMY
Sixth Edition

Thomas Mayer
James S. Duesenberry
Robert Z. Aliber

by
Steven Beckman
University of Colorado

Janet Wolcutt Dimmen
Wichita State University

W. W. Norton & Company
New York   London

Composition by Roberta Flechner Graphics.

ISBN 0-393-96849-9 (pbk.)

W. W. Norton & Company, Inc., 500 Fifth Avenue, New York, N.Y. 10110
W. W. Norton & Company, Ltd., 10 Coptic Street, London WC1A 1PU

1 2 3 4 5 6 7 8 9 0

Contents

Part Four: Monetary Policy   189

Part Five: The International Monetary System   250

Preface

This study guide is designed to help you understand the material presented in *Money, Banking, and the Economy*, Sixth Edition, by Thomas Mayer, James S. Duesenberry, and Robert Z. Aliber. Each chapter in the study guide corresponds to one in the text and provides an extensive array of review questions and exercises intended to make you a more active reader. The more time you spend with the textbook and study guide the better, but you will get the maximum benefit from your reading if you approach each chapter in the following way:

1. Read the Learning Objectives and the Key Terms, Concepts, and Institutions. You now know the main points and key terms to watch for as you read the text.

2. Now read the text. Look for the main points in section headings and key terms in boldface type.

3. Try the Self-Tests. These are designed to reinforce what you read and to test your recall of facts and concepts.

4. Take a break. If you try to do more at this point, diminishing returns set in! Do something else, and let your mind absorb what you have learned.

5. Try the Topics for Discussion. This section turns the major points covered in the chapter into questions or applies the points to current situations.

6. The Exercise Questions are the acid test. If you can get the right numerical answer or correctly identify the critical points, you are well on your way to mastering the material. These sections are also used to show practical applications, such as how to read bond-market quotations or how to calculate the value of an investment.

7. Some material that we have found helpful for our students has also been included. In Chapter 13, the deposit multipliers are given a closer look

in a simple way. In Chapter 28, the key differences between the monetarists and Keynesians are presented in a point-counterpoint format.

Answers are provided at the end of each chapter for the Self-Tests and Exercise Questions, so that these parts of the guide are largely self-contained. Of course, you will have to read the text to respond to the material in Learning Objectives, Key Terms, and Topics for Discussion. If this study guide helps you to get a better feel for what you understand and what you have to work on, then it has accomplished its purpose. Enjoy your studies!

Steven Beckman
Janet Wolcutt Dimmen

Acknowledgments

We want to thank two teachers who have been important to us, Thomas Mayer of the University of California, Davis, and Edward Kane of Ohio State University. For their help in commenting on a previous edition, we also want to thank E. Dwight Phaup of Union College and, again, Thomas Mayer.

Study Guide to Accompany

MONEY, BANKING, AND THE ECONOMY
Sixth Edition

CHAPTER 1   Money

Learning Objectives

1. Understand the importance of money.

2. Distinguish between money, currency, wealth, and income.

3. Understand how a monetary system evolves from a barter system.

4. Describe the four functions of money.

5. List the components of *M-1* (narrow money) and *M-2* (broad money).

6. Explain the difference between credit money and commodity money.

7. Define liquidity and list the three factors that affect an asset's liquidity.

Key Terms, Concepts, and Institutions

money
income
standard of value
barter
transaction costs
full-bodied commodity money
credit money
near-money
double coincidence of wants
trade good
narrow money
point-of-sale terminal

broad money
wealth
medium of exchange
store of wealth
indirect barter
M-1
representative full-bodied money
legal tender, or fiat money
liquidity
standard of deferred payments
M-2

Self-Test: Completion

1. Money whose value as a commodity is equal to its value as money is

    _____ .

2. A token that is accepted in exchange only because others will accept it is

    _____ .

3. In the United States only _____ is legal tender.

4. The acceptance of a commodity in trade because it can be traded relatively easily is _____ .

5. Any commodity or concept used to express prices is a _____ .

6. Whatever is routinely accepted in trade is a _____ .

7. _____ includes items that are highly liquid but are excluded from our definition of money.

8. Currency plus checkable deposits can be referred to as _____ .

9. Some believe governments and credit money are a dangerous combination because governments may be tempted to expand the supply of credit money rapidly and this would lead to _____ .

10. In the short run, raising the quantity of money rapidly has very pleasant results: _____ falls.

Self-Test: True-False

T 1. Money is important because any breakdown in the money system has chain-reaction consequences in the exchange and production systems. If payment is difficult, so are sales and production.

T 2. The evolution of money has been from concrete objects to abstract symbols.

F 3. Corporate stock is near-money.

F 4. Credit money has no value.

T 5. Inflation may result from excessive money growth.

T 6. All U.S. money is credit money.

F 7. Narrow money includes currency, traveler's checks, checkable deposits, and savings and time deposits of $100,000 or less.

T 8. Wire transfers of deposits account for the bulk of monetary transactions.

T 9. The medium-of-exchange function becomes more important as the economy becomes more specialized.

T 10. If X can be bought or sold quickly and easily with no transactions costs and the price of X does not change however long the buyer or seller searches for a better deal, then X is perfectly liquid.

T 11. In the last days of the Soviet Union, the increase in the supply of money would not have resulted in barter if prices had been allowed to rise.

Self-Test: Multiple Choice

1. Some believe commodity money is better than credit money because
    a. it is irrational to accept tokens in exchange for goods and services.
    b. the supply of credit money is often manipulated by governments to achieve short-term goals.
    c. the supply of commodity money never varies.
    d. commodity money is more efficient in that it uses fewer resources.
    e. all the above.

2. Which of the following is not a medium of exchange?
    a. coin
    b. currency
    c. checkable deposits
    d. wire transfers
    e. passbook savings accounts

3. Which of the following is not a component of broad money?
    a. currency
    b. time deposits of $100,000 or less
    c. stocks
    d. checkable deposits
    e. traveler's checks

4. Barter may replace money if
    a. inflation is rampant.
    b. prices are controlled.
    c. taxes are excessive.
    d. only credit money exists.
    e. all but d.

5. Which of the following is the most liquid?
    a. coin and currency
    b. bonds

    c.   a house

    d.   a passbook savings account

    e.   stocks

6.   Money and income are
    a.   the same since more money is more income.
    b.   the same since we measure income in dollars.
    c.   different since money refers to the current holdings of media of exchange, while income refers to the value of resources received in a given period of time.
    d.   different since money can be inherited but income is earned.
    e.   different since money is savings and income equals expenditures.

7.   In a modern economy, barter may be used when
    a.   a gigantic inflation occurs.
    b.   there is a high degree of specialization and division of labor.
    c.   prices ar enot permitted to adjust to equilibrium.
    d.   all the above.
    e.   only *a* and *c.*

8.   Which of the following is a problem associated with the use of barter?
    a.   Transactions costs are low.
    b.   Barter encourages specialization.
    c.   Barter eliminates the need for a double coincidence of wants.
    d.   Barter encourages the division of labor.
    e.   Some goods are not divisible.

9.   Inflation undermines money as
    a.   a standard of value.
    b.   thae standard of deferred payment.
    c.   a store of wealth.
    d.   a medium of exchange.
    e.   all the above.

10.   Credit money
    a.   economizes on scarce resources but its supply is controlled by accidental discoveries.
    b.   implies that a loan has been made.
    c.   is controlled by government, and this may or may not be good.
    d.   is no longer in routine use.
    e.   has been compared to bicycle locks of case-hardened steel.

Topics for Discussion

1.   Describe the evolution from barter to indirect barter to the use of money.

2. Compare the transaction costs of storing wealth as money with storing it as stocks and bonds.

3. Give an example where more than one monetary unit has been used to fulfill the three functions of money.

4. Describe how computer-based technology could change our conception of money.

5. In what sense is money a poor store of value?

Exercise Questions

1. Imagine an economy made up of the people and goods in Table 1.1 below. Each column refers to the good listed at the top and each row to the person listed at the left. A positive entry indicates the number of units of the good that someone has and is willing to sell. A negative entry indicates the number of units of the good that the person wants to buy. Each of these entries refers to either the quantities supplied or demanded given a price of 1 dollar for each good. For example, Gerry has two bushels of potatoes to sell. He wants to buy 2 hours of child guidance for his daughter.

    Notice that all the rows and columns add up to zero. That means we have an equilibrium price system. Each person is able to trade for what he or she wants and the quantities demanded and supplied are equal at the given prices.

Table 1.1   A Sample Economy

	Potatoes	Dance lessons	Child guidance
Gerry, the potato farmer	+2	0	−2
Jan, the dance instructor	−2	+2	0
Martin, the child psychologist	0	−2	+2

    a. Assume Gerry has two dollars. Construct a set of money-using trades that clears the market.

    b. Construct a set of barter or indirect barter transactions that clears the market. Remember that services such as dance lessons or child guidance cannot be passed through an intermediary.

2. The act of saving is very different in a monetary system than in a barter system. In a barter system, if Jan wants to save a potato, she simply sets it aside. In a monetary system, she would buy one less potato. So, at existing prices the quantity supplied of potatoes would be (*a.* greater than/equal to/less than) the quantity demanded. The price of potatoes

would (*b.* rise/fall/not change). When she chooses to spend her money on potatoes in the next period, the price of potatoes would tend to (*c.* rise/fall).

Therefore, under a barter system, Jan's decision to save (*d.* increases/decreases/does not affect) Gerry's income. Under a monetary system, Jan's decision to save (*e.* raises/lowers/does not affect) Gerry's current income but it (*f.* raises/lowers/does not affect) Gerry's future income.

The simple Keynesian model predicts that consumption and current income will fall if savings increase. This makes sense in a (*g.* barter/monetary) system where the effects on future income are (*h.:* considered/ignored). This illustrates the connection between money and recessions as well as the need for money in a complex, highly specialized, service-oriented society.

3. Match the function of money with the example that illustrates that function.

   a.   medium of exchange
   b.   standard of value
   c.   standard of deferred payment
   d.   store of wealth

   1. *b* A "help wanted" advertisement states that new hires will start at $6.95 per hour.
   2. *d* Alice puts a $100 bill in an envelope in her dresser drawer in July which she plans to use in December to buy a Christmas gift for her grandson.
   3. *a* Mr. LaMarr gives Jason Smith $10 for mowing his lawn.
   4. *c* Mr. and Mrs. Clark want to buy a new sports car. They sign a car loan agreement which states that they will pay the Campus Credit Union $545 a month for five years.

4.   ELAEIS, Ivory Coast—Standing in his rubber plantation here, Fulgence Koffy describes the lean years. "I was losing money on every kilogram of rubber I sold, and I feared I was going under," he recalls. "Then, overnight, the price doubled, and the loss became a profit." . . .
      Sitting in his rector's office in the University of Yaounde in Cameroon, Dominique Obounou Akong talks about an elusive fax machine. "One day, I had enough money to buy it," he says. "The next day, I had the same amount of money—but it only bought half a fax. . . ."
      Both stories stem from the 1994 devaluation of the CFA franc, a currency shared by 14 African countries. . . . *Wall Street Journal,* 10, 1995, p. 1A.

   Which of the four functions of money have been undermined by the devaluation of the CFA franc?

Answers to Self-Tests

Completion

1.	commodity money	6.	medium of exchange
2.	credit money	7.	near-money
3.	currency	8.	*M-1*
4.	indirect barter	9.	inflation
5.	standard of value	10.	unemployment

True-False

1.	True	7.	False
2.	True	8.	True
3.	False	9.	True
4.	False	10.	True
5.	True	11.	True
6.	True		

Multiple Choice

1.	*b*	6.	*c*
2.	*e*	7.	*e*
3.	*c*	8.	*e*
4.	*e*	9.	*e*
5.	*a*	10.	*c*

Answers to Exercise Questions

1. *a.* Gerry uses his 2 dollars to buy two hours of child psychology from Martin. Martin uses the same 2 dollars to buy two hours of dance instruction from Jan. Jan uses the same 2 dollars to buy 2 bushels of potatoes from Gerry.

    b. Notice that no double coincidence of wants exists. Someone will have to accept a good in trade that they do not want in order to trade for what they do want. Next, since services like child psychology cannot be passed from one person to the next, this system does not have even an indirect barter solution unless Martin can be convinced to accept potatoes that he does not want. Martin trades his service for 2 units of Gerry's potatoes. He then gives the potatoes to Jan in return for dance instruction. If Martin fails to see the opportunity, the others are powerless to act.

2.
a.	greater than	*e.*	lowers
b.	fall	*f.*	raises
c.	rise	*g.*	monetary
d.	does not affect	*h.*	ignored

3. *a.* 3   *c.* 4
    b. 1   *d.* 2

4. All the functions of money are undermined to some extent. Mr. Akong's story illustrates how the CFA franc lost its usefulness as a store of value due to the devaluation. Mr. Koffy's story is an example of the change in the CFA franc in its function as a standard of value.

CHAPTER 2 Stocks, Bonds, and Financial Institutions

Learning Objectives

1. Describe the intermediation function of financial intermediaries.
2. Distinguish between debt and equity instruments.
3. Explain why bond prices fall when interest rates rise.
4. Identify the demanders and suppliers of funds.
5. Explain why the extra cost of a firm's new loan is greater than the interest rate on the loan.
6. Identify the three benefits of financial intermediation.
7. List the major types of financial intermediation and their functions.
8. List four reasons for government regulation of financial institutions.

Key Terms, Concepts, and Institutions

financial system	credit unions
claims	stockbrokers
division of labor	investment banks
equity	syndicate
debt	underwriting
partnerships	security dealers
corporation	private pension funds
residual claimant	mutual funds
bond	load funds
maturity	no-load funds
duration	nondepository institutions
coupon rate	money-market mutual funds

call protection	casualty companies
preferred stock	finance companies
convertible bonds	federal credit agencies
mathematical value	Federal National Mortgage Association
face value	(Fannie Mae)
agents	Government National Mortgage
retailers	Association (Ginnie Mae)
insurers	Federal Home Loan Mortgage
financial intermediaries	Corporation (Freddie Mac)
consumer ignorance	Banks for Cooperatives
depository institutions	Federal Intermediate Credit Banks
commercial banks	Federal Land Banks
savings and loan associations	Federal Housing Administration
mutual savings banks	Veterans Administration
life insurance companies	

Self-Test: Completion

1. Proprietorships and partnerships are exposed to the risk that business losses may have to be covered by personal assets. _____ avoid this risk.

2. Corporate stockholders are paid only after all interest obligations on debt have been met. Stockholders are _____ claimants.

3. Issuing new stock will be advantageous to existing stockholders if the additional profits per dollar of stock issued are _____ than the current average profit per dollar of stock. (Put differently, average profits rise if marginal profits are _____ .)

4. If interest rates increase, the prices of existing bonds will _____ .

5. _____ issue claims on themselves that are fixed in dollar terms.

6. _____ stock is stock on which the corporation has to pay a minimum dividend before it is allowed to pay a dividend to common-stock holders.

7. Convertible bonds pay a _____ interest rate than comparable regular bonds.

8. The value at which the bond was initially issued is called its

   _____ value.

9. A clause that limits the right of early repayment of a bond is called

   _____ _____ .

10. Usually, the higher the yield on a security, the _____ its risk.

11. _____ banks do not take deposits.

12. _____ represents ownership; _____ represent debt.

Self-Test: True-False

F 1. The coupon rate on a bond rises and falls with average returns on the stock market.

T 2. The mathematical value of an asset is a kind of average. For example, if there is a 10 percent chance of a $100 loss and a 90 percent chance of a $100 gain, then the mathematical value is $90 − $10 = $80.

F 3. Stockholders of a corporation are liable for its debts.

F 4. Investment banks take deposits.

F 5. Securities dealers operate on the primary market.

T 6. Money-market mutual funds invest clients' funds in a pool of liquid, safe, short-term securities and often offer limited check-writing services.

F 7. Insurance company investments are principally short term.

F 8. Professional mutual fund managers consistently outperform the market as a whole.

T 9. If interest rates paid to depositors remain constant while other interest rates fall, the decisions by depositors of whether to withdraw deposits are not independent of each other.

F 10. Corporate bonds are more liquid than a deposit in a savings and loan association.

T 11. The yield on a typical bond is much more certain than the yield on stock.

F 12. State and local government securities are considered to be riskless, since these governmental units can always raise taxes to pay off their debts.

⊤ 13. The intermediation function of financial intermediaries is to bring savers and borrowers together.

⊤ 14. One rationale for government regulation of financial intermediaries is that consumers do not have the expertise to evaluate the soundness of the institutions.

Self-Test: Multiple Choice

1. Which statement about insurance companies is false?
   a. They invest primarily in liquid assets.
   b. They administer pension funds.
   c. They make contingent payments.
   d. They can be organized as stock or mutual companies.
   e. They sell annuities.

2. Which of the following will not benefit if a corporation's stock goes up?
   a. A holder of common stock.
   b. A bondholder.
   c. The holder of a convertible bond.
   d. The holder of preferred stock.
   e. None of the above; all benefit when the price of a corporation's stock increases.

3. A security has a 30 percent chance of paying 20 percent, a 35 percent chance of paying 25 percent, and a 35 percent chance of paying −10 percent. What is its mathematical value?
   a. 18.25 percent
   b. 14.75 percent
   c. 11.25 percent
   d. 45.00 percent
   e. 35.00 percent

4. Which of the following sectors of the economy are not suppliers of funds?
   a. Households.
   b. Business firms.
   c. The federal government.
   d. State and local governments.
   e. None of the above; all supply funds.

5. Financial intermediaries
   a. sell claims on others.
   b. reduce liquidity.

    c.   have enough funds on hand to pay off depositors.

    ⓓ   reduce risk by pooling loans.

    e.   have no influence over the money supply.

6.   It is sometimes argued that the government provides credit, rather than relying on the market, because

    a.   home ownership is a valuable national resource.

    b.   special interest groups lobby for this goody from government.

    c.   subsidizing credit by providing loan guarantees is off the budget.

    d.   farmers' credit needs are not met by private firms.

    ⓔ   all the above.

7.   A bond with a face value of $1,000 and a coupon rate of 10 percent pays _____ annually and will sell for _____ if interest rates have risen since the date of issue.

    ⓐ $100, less than $1,000

    b. $50, less than $1,000

    c. $100, more than $1,000

    d. $50, more than $1,000

    e.   varying amounts, precisely $1,000

8.   Which of the following can issue equity securities?

    a.   households

    ⓑ   businesses

    c.   state governments

    d.   local governments

    e.   the federal government

9.   Which of the following exhibits the lowest degree of risk?

    a.   corporate bonds

    ⓑ   U.S. government bonds

    c.   corporate stock

    d.   commercial paper

    e.   municipal bonds

10.   According to the text, justifications for regulating banks and other financial intermediaries include

    a.   consumers are ignorant.

    b.   bank failures can result in a catastrophic reduction in the money supply.

    c.   regulation is an effective way to reallocate resources.

    d.   there are extensive economies of scale in banking.

    ⓔ   a and b.

11. Financial intermediaries can borrow short term to lend long term because
    a. long-term interest rates are higher than short-term interest rates.
    b. financial intermediaries generally have inside information about the stock market.
    c. if a group of depositors is large, their demand for cash is predictable.
    d. information and transactions costs are smaller for financial intermediaries than they are for depositors.
    e. government regulations encourage them to do so.

12. Which of the following is not a depository institution?
    a. a commercial bank
    b. a pension fund
    c. a savings and loan
    d. a credit union
    e. a mutual savings bank

13. Which of the following is not a federal agency dealing with the housing sector?
    a. GNMA
    b. FNMA
    c. FHLMC
    d. FHA
    e. GMAC

Topics for Discussion

1. A broker performs a pure search function by bringing potential borrowers and lenders together and receives a fee or commission for this service. Unlike a dealer, a broker does not take legal possession of the claims traded. Are the broker's services an intermediation activity as defined by the text? Be prepared to defend your answer.

2. Explain why financial intermediaries can reduce costs.

3. Give an example of a circumstance where the decisions of depositors will not be independent of each other, so that depository institutions will not be able to predict deposit outflows accurately.

4. Suppose that you anticipate that the rate of inflation will increase to 10 percent this year. Would you rather be a lender holding a $5,000 bond that pays a fixed 8 percent interest or the borrower who issued the bond? Be prepared to defend your answer.

5. Do you think the capacity of financial intermediaries to devise new instruments makes regulation easier or more difficult?

6. U.S. businesses have been criticized for being overly concerned with short-term performance. What kind of financial structure encourages long-run planning?

Exercise Questions

1. Assume a market for a one-year security in which borrowers and lenders deal directly with each other. The observed rate at which the security is traded is 12 percent.

    a. Since both the borrower and the lender incur costs in seeking each other out, the 12 percent rate (is/is not) the effective cost to the borrower (and/or) the effective return to the lender.

    b. A premium is the compensation that an economic unit receives to induce it to bear a particular type of risk. Assume equal information and transactions costs to both the borrower and the lender of 4 percent. Since the lender is taking the risk that the borrower will

    not be able to repay the loan, assume a _____ premium of 2 percent to compensate the lender for the risk of default. Since the lender's funds will be tied up for a year, assume a liquidity premium of 1 percent is necessary to compensate the lender for this loss of liquidity. The effective return to the lender (the actual return plus any implicit benefits and minus any implicit costs) is the observed rate (plus/minus) information and transactions costs, the default premium, and the liquidity premium. The effective cost to the borrower is the observed rate (plus/minus) information and transactions costs.
    Without intermediation, the effective rate of return to the

    lender is _____ percent, and the effective cost to the

    borrower is _____ percent.

2. A financial intermediary is set up to collect the funds of savers and make loans to borrowers, so we would expect information and transactions costs to be (*a:* greater/less) for the financial intermediary than for individual borrowers and savers.

    b. Assume the information and transactions costs are 1 percent for the Uriskit National Bank. Uriskit also has a lower default premium, about 1 percent, due to its expertise in credit evaluation and its ability to pool risk. Uriskit's funds will be tied up for one year in this security, so assume a liquidity premium of 1 percent. Because Uriskit is a profit-motivated institution, it charges a fee of 1 percent for its services. Then the rate that Uriskit could pay to lenders (depositors) is the going rate of 12 percent (plus/minus) information costs and transactions costs, the default

and liquidity premiums, and its fee, or _____ percent.

c.   This rate (is/is not) the effective rate of return to the lender, because the lender still incurs information and transaction costs even if a financial intermediary is used. However, these costs are usually substantially (more/less) than if they had dealt directly with the borrower. Likewise, the lender still has some default risk and loses some liquidity, but again these premiums will be less than if the lender had dealt directly with the borrower. Assume that, by going through the financial intermediary, information and transactions costs are reduced to 1 percent for both the borrower and the lender, and the default and liquidity premiums to the lender are reduced to $1/2$ percent each.

   If the borrower and the lender go through a financial

intermediary, the effective return to the lender is _____ percent.

   If the borrower and the lender go through a financial intermediary, the net cost to the borrower is the observed rate

(plus/minus) information and transaction costs, or _____ percent.

   Using the financial intermediary (increased/decreased) the effective return to the lender and (increased/decreased) the effective cost to the borrower.

3.   The following exercise is designed to illustrate the advantages of diversification and risk-pooling.

Suppose that you have $10,000 to invest and three options:
   Option *a:* You can buy a U.S. government security that offers a guaranteed return of 8 percent.
   Option *b:* You can buy one of three private loans offering a 15 percent rates of return. One of these will default, but you don't know which one. Each loan therefore has a $2/3$ chance of a 15 percent return, and a $1/3$ chance of a 0 percent return.
   Option *c:* You can pool your money with three other investors, buy all four assets, and split the earnings.

What is the mathematical value of the dollar amount of return for each option?

    Option *a:* $

    Option *b:* $

    Option *c:* $

Discuss the relevant risk and return of each option.

4.   If the market interest rate on a bond is *i*, the present value (PV) of the payment (*A*) to be received at maturity, which is *t* years in the future, is given by the formula

$$PV = \frac{A}{(1+i)^t}.$$

An investor would be willing to pay the present value (or less) to buy the bond today.

  a. Suppose that you buy a five-year bond that has a maturity value of $5,000 and the market interest rate is 8 percent. What is the highest price that you would be willing to pay for this bond?

  b. Suppose that the day after you buy the bond, the market interest rate rises to 10 percent. If you had to sell the bond in a hurry to raise cash, what is the highest price you can expect to receive?

     As the market interest rate rises, the prices of bonds (rise/fall).

  c. Suppose you keep the bond for three years, and then sell it. If the market interest rate stayed at 8 percent, what is the highest price you can expect to receive for this bond with two years remaining to maturity?

     As the length of time to maturity decreases, the prices of bonds (increase/decrease).

5.   Here is an example of how financial information is reported in the newspapers. All the quotations are from the *Wall Street Journal.*

Bond-Market Information

Bonds	Cur yld	Vol	Close	Net chg.
Sears 9½ 99	8.6	51	111	+³⁄₈

    First, you see the name of the company that issued the bond, in this case Sears. The 9½ is the coupon yield, and the 99 means the bond will mature in 1999. Each bond has a face (or par) value printed on it. Sears will pay the holder of the bond $1,000 of

principal for each $1,000 of face value when the bond matures in
1999. Sears will also pay 9¹/₂ percent, or $95.00 annually (usually
in semi-annual installments) for each $1,000 of face value.

To conserve space, bond prices are stated as a percentage of 100,
with 100 representing the $1,000 face value. Here, the closing price
for the day was $1,110.00. This closing price was up ³/₈ percent
from the previous day's closing price, or $3.75.

The current yield refers to the dollar return per year divided by
the current market price. If the bond pays $95.00 per year and has a
price of $1,110.00, the current yield is .08558, or about 8.6 percent.
Note that the current yield is different from the coupon yield, since
the current price is not equal to the maturity value.

Look at the following quotation:

Bonds	Cur yld	Vol	Close	Net chg.
GnEl 8¹/₂ 04	?	30	76¹/₂	+³/₄

   a.   Who issued the bond?

   b.   What is the coupon yield? What is the dollar amount (per $1,000 of face value) of the coupon payment?

   c.   What is the current yield?

   d.   What was the closing price the day before?

  6.   Here is another example of how financial information is reported.

Stock-Market Information

| 52 weeks | | | | Yld | | | Vol | | | | Net |
High	Low	Stock	Div.	(%)	PE	100s	High	Low	Close	chg.
40	28¹/₂	Exxon	3.20	8.7	6	6342	37	36¹/₂	36³/₄	+³/₈

Exxon issued this stock, which pays an annual dividend of $3.20. The
dividend is compared with the current price to get the current yield. The
closing price was 36³/₄, or $36.75. To get the current yield, we divide $3.20
by $36.75 to get .0870748, or 8.7 percent. The PE is the price per share
divided by the earnings per share. For a given stock price, the lower the PE
ratio, the higher the earnings. The Vol-100s column tells us the number of
shares traded on that particular day. The High and Low columns to the right
of the company name tell us the high and low prices for that day. The High
and Low columns to the left of the company name give the high and low
prices for the stock for the preceding 52 weeks.

Look at the quotation below.

52 weeks		Stock	Div.	Yld (%)	PE Ratio	Vol 100s	High	Low	Close	Net chg.
High	Low									
36⅞	21⅜	Avon	2	?	11	1321	24⅞	24⅝	24¾	−⅛

    a.   What is the name of the issuing company?

    b.   What is the current yield?

    c.   Was this stock traded more actively than Exxon on this particular day?

    d.   What was the lowest price at which you could have bought Avon stock in the last year?

    e.   What was the closing price the day before?

7.   WASHINGTON—Despite the obvious weakening of the U.S. economy, the Federal Reserve isn't likely to cut short-term interest rates anytime soon. . . .

    The Fed's policy-making Open-Market Committee is widely expected to hold interest rates steady when it meets behind closed doors here on May 23, but analysts are divided about whether the Fed will raise or lower rates later this year . . . *Wall Street Journal*, May 12, 1995, p. A2.

If the Fed does choose to lower interest rates later this year, we would expect bond prices to (rise/fall), all other things being equal.

8. For each of the following financial intermediaries, circle "D" if the institution is a depository institution, and "ND" if it is not a depository institution. Then list the main types of assets each institution holds.

Financial institution	Nature	Main types of assests held
Commercial banks	D ND	
Credit unions	D ND	
Life insurance companies	D ND	
Mutual funds	D ND	
Mutual savings banks	D ND	
Other insurance companies	D ND	
Pension funds	D ND	
Savings and loans	D ND	

Answers to Self-Tests

Completion

1. Corporations
2. residual
3. higher; higher
4. decrease
5. depository institutions
6. Preferred
7. lower
8. face
9. call protection
10. higher
11. investment
12. Equity or stocks; bonds

True-False

1. False
2. True
3. False
4. False
5. False
6. True
7. False
8. False
9. True
10. False
11. True
12. False
13. True
14. True

Multiple Choice

1. a
2. b
3. c
4. e
5. d
6. e
7. a
8. b
9. b
10. e
11. c
12. b
13. e

Answers to Exercise Questions

1. a. is not, or
   b. default; minus; plus; 5, 16

2. a. less
   b. minus, 8
   c. is not; less; 6; plus, 13; increased, decreased

3. Option *a:* 8 percent of $10,000 = $800. This option is riskless.

   Option *b:* You have a $2/3$ chance of receiving 15 percent of $10,000, or $1,500, and a $1/3$ chance of receiving nothing. Your mathematical value, or expected rate of return, is $2/3(\$1,500) + 1/3(0) = \$1,000$.

Option *c:* Your group buys the government bond and gets $800 and the three bonds, one of which goes sour. Your group gets 15 percent of $10,000 from each of the two good bonds, and nothing from the one that fails. You get $800 + $3,000 = $3,800 altogether, or $950 each. Each of you accepted a small certain loss to protect yourself against the possibility of a greater loss.

4.   *a.* $\$5{,}000/(1 + .08)^5 = \$3{,}402.92$.
      b. $\$5{,}000/(1 + .10)^5 = \$3{,}104.61$; fall.
      c. $\$5{,}000/(1 + .08)^2 = \$4{,}286.69$; increase.

5.   *a.*   General Electric
      b.   8.5 percent; $85
      c.   11.1 percent
      d. $765 – $7.50 = $757.50

6.   *a.*   Avon
      b.   8.08 percent
      c.   no
      d. $21.38
      e. $24.875

7.   rise

8.

Financial institution	Nature	Main types of assests held
Commercial banks	(D) ND	Mortgages, commercial loans, consumer loans, debt securities
Credit unions	(D) ND	Consumer loans, mortagage loans
Life insurance companies	D (ND)	Stocks and bonds, real estate
Mutual funds	D (ND)	Treasury bills, commercial paper, stocks, bonds
Mutual savings banks	(D) ND	Mortgages, U.S. government securities
Other insurance companies	D (ND)	Stocks and bonds, real estate
Pension funds	D (ND)	Stocks and bonds
Savings and loans	(D) ND	Mortgages, U.S. government securities

CHAPTER 3   Financial Theory

Learning Objectives

1. Evaluate a portfolio in terms of yield and risk.

2. Describe hedging strategies to reduce or eliminate diversifiable risk and interest-rate risk.

3. Describe the characteristics of an asset that determine its value.

4. Explain the Modigliani-Miller theorem, the Capital Asset Pricing Model, and the principal-agent problem.

5. Assess the performance of capital markets in terms of the efficient-markets theory, moral hazard, asymmetric information, and signaling.

Key Terms, Concepts, and Institutions

signaling

moral hazard

adverse selection

asymmetric information

portfolio

yield

risk

variance

purchasing-power risk

interest-rate risk

default risk

CAPM

beta

behavioral theory of finance

portfolio risk

hedging

contingent claims

diversifiable risk

Modigliani-Miller theorem

variable-rate loan

efficient-markets theory

securitization

interest-rate swaps

stripping

contingent interest rates

Self-Test: Completion

1. We use expected value to measure the average value of an asset and
   _____ (a measure of the dispersion about the average) as a
   partial guide to risk.

2. Someone who lends the $10,000 she intends to use to buy a car takes the
   risk that the price of the car she wants may rise substantially. This is
   _____ risk.

3. Since people can either buy stock or bonds, they must be indifferent
   between the two options in equilibrium. This is the core idea behind the
   _____ .

4. Contracts that allow corporations to make payments on each other's
   loans are called _____ .

5. If a bond's capital gains go to one set of investors and its interest
   payments to another, then that bond has been _____ .

6. Many financial intermediaries do not retain possession of the loans they
   originate but sell ownership shares in bundles of like loans on the open
   market. This is called _____ .

7. Usually, the higher the yield on a security, the _____ its risk.

8. The collection of assets one owns is called a _____ .

9. _____ is the risk that the borrower may simply declare
   bankruptcy and not pay the principal or interest.

10. _____ is the risk that the sales price of the security will fall.

11. Revenues that become receivable if an event occurs, such as life
    insurance, are called _____ .

12. According to _____ , stock prices are a random walk.

13. The tendency for the insured to take greater risk is called _____ .

14. Stockbrokers earn commissions based on the value of transactions and
    therefore have an incentive to advise clients to buy and sell frequently.
    This is an example of _____ .

15. The beta coefficient measures how volatile a stock is relative to the
    _____ stock.

Self-Test: True-False

т 1. The expected value of an asset is a kind of average. For example, if there is a 10 percent chance of a $100 loss and a 90 percent chance of a $100 gain, then the expected value is $90 – $10 = $80.

F 2. Someone who provides for his retirement by buying a long-term bond at a fixed interest rate avoids purchasing-power risk.

F 3. Stock yields have to be high to compensate for diversifiable risk.

F 4. There can be risk only if losses are possible.

F 5. Investors demand a higher return the higher the diversifiable risk.

т 6. If bank stock becomes riskier, then the price of nonbank stock should rise.

т 7. Capital markets work to reduce the differences in the marginal disutility of risk-bearing between investors.

F 8. Interest payments and dividend payments may be deducted from taxes.

т 9. Wide swings in stock prices, such as the October 1987 stock market crash, are taken as evidence against the efficient-markets theory.

F 10. The process of brokerage firms guaranteeing mortgages is called "securitization."

F 11. A low-risk portfolio contains only assets that individually have small risk.

т 12. The fact that the weather in New York affects stock prices suggests human behavior and moods affect asset valuation.

F 13. Banks give loans to whoever is willing to pay the highest rate of interest.

Self-Test: Multiple Choice

1. The demand for an asset will rise as
   a. liquidity decreases.
   b. yields on competing assets increase.
   c. the variance of the asset's yield decreases.
   d. the correlation of the asset's yield with competing assets increases.
   e. wealth declines.

2. Which two assets when held together are a good hedge against risk?
   a. loans to General Motors and construction firms in Detroit (Consider regional risk.)

b. stock in oil companies and recreation vehicle manufacturers (Consider OPEC risk.)

c. stock in oil and coal companies (Consider OPEC risk.)

d. stock in refrigerator manufacturers and auto manufacturers (Consider recession risk.)

e. stocks and long-term bonds (Consider purchasing power risk.)

3. In the 1980s corporations shifted toward bond finance because
   a. capital gains taxes were reduced.
   b. the wave of leveraged buyouts increased stock prices.
   c. personal income taxes fell.
   d. bonds are now insured against purchasing-power risk.
   e. bonds are more likely than stocks to realize capital gains.

4. Corporations that finance long-term projects with short-term loans
   a. usually pay more interest as short-term rates generally exceed long-term rates.
   b. are exposed to interest-rate risk as the project may have to be financed at higher rates in the future.
   c. are fully exposed to purchasing-power risk.
   d. avoid capital gains taxes.
   e. violate the Modigliani-Miller theorem.

5. Financial intermediaries
   a. sell claims on others.
   b. reduce liquidity.
   c. have enough funds on hand to pay off depositors.
   d. reduce risk by pooling loans.
   e. have no influence over the money supply.

6. The efficient-markets theory
   a. means it does not matter what you invest in.
   b. argues that if some asset had a higher expected return or lower expected risk than other assets, its price would be bid up until only a normal expected return for the risk was available.
   c. claims no one can make a killing in the stock market.
   d. can explain the January effect and the value-line anomaly.

7. Which of the following exhibits the lowest degree of default risk?
   a. corporate bonds
   b. U.S. government bonds
   c. corporate stock
   d. commercial paper
   e. municipal bonds

8. Moral hazard
    a. is not much of a problem as long as both parties to the contract have equal information.
    b. is a problem only with dishonest borrowers.
    c. refers to the higher divorce rate and the consequent effect on credit ratings.
    d. became less of a problem due to corporate takeovers.
    e. is also referred to as the Madonna effect.

9. Asymmetric information refers to the
    a. fact that the owner of the used car knows more about the car than the prospective buyer.
    b. tendency entrepreneurs have of candidly assessing the risks and the opportunities of the venture they wish to pursue.
    c. tendency to use brand names to unload shoddy goods.
    d. preference banks have for customers willing to pay high interest rates.
    e. tendency of corporations with high bond ratings to be poor targets for a corporate raider.

10. A corporation interested in signaling high expected profits might
    a. issue stock.
    b. reinvest an unusually high percentage of its earnings.
    c. borrow at very high interest rates.
    d. have a high debt to equity ratio.
    e. reinvest an unusually low percentage of its earnings.

11. The capital assets pricing model argues that an asset's yield depends on
    a. the undiversifiable risk.
    b. the weather in New York.
    c. whether the stock has been rising or falling in value.
    d. a weighted average of potential gains and losses with losses' being given a higher weight.
    e. inflation.

12. According to the Modigliani-Miller theorem,
    a. transactions costs do not matter.
    b. everyone is equally willing to bear risk.
    c. creditors and stockholders, in equilibrium, are equally willing to bear an additonal unit of risk.
    d. firms worry about going bankrupt and therefore prefer bond to stock finance.
    e. tax laws that favor capital gains make bonds preferable to stock.

Topics for Discussion

1. Asymmetric information leads to underfinance of highly risky projects that might be well worth financing. Does this imply government, either state or federal, should use the money in retirement plans to fund such ventures?

2. It is currently difficult to hedge inflation. Should the government perform the service of offering bonds that pay a guaranteed real interest rate (that is, if inflation rises, the nominal rate on the government security rises)?

3. U.S. businesses have been criticized for being overly concerned with short-term performance. What kind of financial structure encourages long-run planning?

4. It is quite likely your school has a computer lab with stock and bond data of some type and various software programs. EVIEWS, RATS, and SAS are common programs and Citibase is the most common data set. Use the software to plot an asset value against time. Apart from a gradual rising trend, there should be no pattern. (Why?)

   However, if you plot exvus and fspcom (citibase names for the exchange rate and the S&P 500), you will probably think you see patterns, especially in the exchange rate. An enormous amount of effort has gone into attempting to reconcile rationality and the patterns we believe we see. What sort of market imperfections, apart from irrationality, could explain patterns?

Exercise Questions

1. Consider the following two assets:

Asset A		Asset B	
Probability	Yield (%)	Probability	Yield (%)
.1	−10	.2	−10
.1	0	.2	0
.6	10	.2	10
.1	20	.2	20
.1	30	.2	30

   a. Calculate the mean expected yields for the two assets.

   b. Use the variance of mean expected yields to calculate the riskiness of each asset.

   c. Use the means and variances to compare the assets.

2. A street vendor can sell either hot dogs or umbrellas or both. Hot dogs yield 12.5 percent when it is sunny, 0 percent if it rains, and umbrellas yield a 50 percent return when it rains, 0 percent otherwise. It is sunny 80 percent of the time.

   a. Calculate the risk and yield for hot dogs and umbrellas.

   b. If the vendor buys $100 worth of umbrellas and $900 worth of hot dogs, what would the risk and yield be for the portfolio?

   c. What main point in the text does the exercise illustrate?

   d. If the vendor wants to eliminate weather risk entirely, how should each $1,000 invested be divided between umbrellas and hot dogs?

Answers to Self-Tests

Completion

1.	variance	9.	Default
2.	purchasing-power	10.	Interest-rate risk
3.	Modigliani-Miller theorem	11.	contingent claims
4.	swaps	12.	efficient-markets theory
5.	stripped	13.	moral hazard
6.	securitization	14.	principal-agent problem
7.	higher	15.	average
8.	portfolio		

True-False

1.	True	8.	False (not dividends)
2.	False	9.	True
3.	False	10.	False
4.	False	11.	False
5.	False	12.	True
6.	True	13.	False
7.	True		

Multiple Choice

1.	c	7.	b
2.	b	8.	a
3.	c	9.	a
4.	b	10.	b
5.	d	11.	a
6.	b	12.	c

Answers to Exercise Questions

1. *a.* The mean expected yields are:

Asset A	Asset B
$.1 \times -10 = -1$	$.2 \times -10 = -2$
$.1 \times 0 = 0$	$.2 \times 0 = 0$
$.6 \times 10 = 6$	$.2 \times 10 = 2$
$.1 \times 20 = 2$	$.2 \times 20 = 4$
$.1 \times 30 = \underline{3}$	$.2 \times 30 = \underline{6}$
10 percent	10 percent

    b. The variances are 100 and 200:

    Asset A

    $.1 \times (-10 - 10)^2 = .1 \times (-20)^2 = .1 \times 400 = 40$
    $.1 \times (0 - 10)^2 = .1 \times (10)^2 = .1 \times 100 = 10$
    $.6 \times (10 - 10)^2 = .6 \times (0)^2 = .6 \times 0 = 0$
    $.1 \times (20 - 10)^2 = .1 \times (10)^2 = .1 \times 100 = 10$
    $.1 \times (30 - 10)^2 = .1 \times (20)^2 = .1 \times 400 = \underline{40}$
    100

    Asset B

    $.2 \times (-10 - 10)^2 = .2 \times (-20)^2 = .2 \times 400 = 80$
    $.2 \times (0 - 10)^2 = .2 \times (10)^2 = .2 \times 100 = 20$
    $.2 \times (-10 - 10)^2 = .2 \times (0)^2 = .2 \times 0 = 0$
    $.2 \times (20 - 10)^2 = .2 \times (10)^2 = .2 \times 100 = 20$
    $.2 \times (30 - 10)^2 = .2 \times (20)^2 = .2 \times 400 = \underline{80}$
    200

    c. While the two assets have the same expected yield, Asset B is riskier.

2. *a.*

Yield	Rain		Shine					Average
Hot dogs	.2(0)	+	.8(12.5)	=	0	+	10	= 10%
Umbrellas	.2(50)	+	.8(0)	=	10%	+	0	= 10%

    Risk

Hot dogs	.2(0 − 10)²	+	.8(12.5 − 10)²	=	25%
Umbrellas	.2(50 − 10)²	+	.8(0 − 10)²	=	400%

    b. In the combined portfolio, if it rains, 10 percent of the money earns 50 percent and 90 percent earns 0 percent, so the expected yield is $(.10) \times (.50) = 5$ percent. Similarly, the expected yield if it shines is 11.25 percent.

	Rain	Shine		Combined
Yield	$.2(50)$	$+ .8(11.25)$	=	10%
Risk	$.2(5-10)^2$	$+ .8(11.25-10)^2$	=	6.25%

c. Adding a small inventory of umbrellas reduces the risk of the portfolio, even though umbrellas by themselves are even riskier! The reason is that when hot dogs do poorly, umbrellas do well. The street vendor has constructed a hedge against weather risk.

d. If $200 of umbrellas and $800 of hotdogs are purchased, then the yield if it rains is $.2(50) = 10$ percent, and the yield if it shines is $.8(12.5) = 10$ percent. The vendor always gets a 10 percent return, rain or shine.

CHAPTER 4   Asset Markets

Learning Objectives

1. Describe the various financial assets, their characteristics, and the markets in which they are traded.

2. Compare and contrast auction versus over-the-counter markets.

3. Explain the organization of the bond, stock, government securities, and foreign-exchange markets.

4. Explain the various instruments used in these financial markets, such as options, forward transactions, futures, and securitized mortgages.

Key Terms, Concepts, and Institutions

over-the-counter or
   telephone market
auction market
real assets
financial assets
open outcry
market in bank deposits
foreign-exchange market
spot transaction
forward transaction
yield curve
securitization
U.S. government securities
put option
derivatives

floaters
call option
strike price
general obligation bonds
revenue bonds
industrial development bonds
U.S. corporate bond market
Euro-bond market
market risk
junk bond
stock price futures
securitized mortgage
wholesale markets
retail markets
reverse floaters

Self-Test: Completion

1. It is generally true that the number of traders allowed in
   ___auction___ markets is limited.

2. If one unit of an asset is a perfect substitute for another unit, trading in
   these assets occurs in a ___wholesale___ market.

3. The buyer of a ___put___ option of a government security has the
   right to sell the security to the option's seller at an agreed-on price
   before an expiration date.

4. The ___Euro -___ bond market evolved largely as a method to evade
   taxes.

5. ___Floaters___ are securities whose interest payments change along with
   the interest rates on newly issued securities.

6. Bonds secured by the general taxing authority of the government issuing
   the bond are ___gen. obligation___ bonds, while bonds secured by the income
   of particular sources are ___revenue___ bonds.

7. New securities created by splitting an original security into its
   component parts are called ___derivatives___.

8. Foreign-exchange contracts negotiated today with the actual currency
   exchange to take place in 30, 60, 90 days or even a year from now are
   ___forward___ transactions.

9. If the buyer of a call option chooses to exercise the option, she
   (pays/receives) the ___strike price___.

10. A mortgage is an example of a ___financial___ asset, while a house is an
    example of a ___real___ asset.

11. Deposits are ___liabilities___ of banks.

12. Spot transactions involve the exchange of deposits within
    ___two___ days after the agreement is reached.

13. The relationship between interest rates on short-term securities and
    interest rates on long-term securities is known as the ___yield___
    curve.

Self-Test: True-False

F 1. If the units of the asset are unique, it is more likely to be traded in wholesale than retail markets.

F 2. More than 90 percent of foreign exchange is traded by the open-outcry method.

T 3. The market for U.S. government bonds is more liquid than the market for state and local government securities.

T 4. Stock index futures allow individuals to buy or sell packages of several stocks at a future date.

F 5. Representatives of buyers and sellers communicate by phone or computer in an auction market.

F 6. The buyer of a put or call option is not required to pay the seller for the option if the option is not exercised.

T 7. If you believe interest rates are about to rise, you might want to buy a put option on a government bond.

F 8. Unlike the market for state and local government securities, the market for U.S. government bonds is an auction market.

T 9. Junk bonds allow relatively unknown corporations access to the bond market.

F 10. An importer who owes 200 million yen in 90 days can avoid the risk that the value of the yen will rise by selling 200 million yen forward.

T 11. Interest rates of the same or highly similar securities in different markets tend to move together.

Self-Test: Multiple Choice

1. Which of the following is sold in a wholesale market?
   a. unimproved land
   b. racehorses
   c. art
   d. rare books
   e. corporate bonds

2. Mortgage debt
   a. is highly illiquid.
   b. can be bundled into packages and traded.
   c. is held by the lender to maturity.

    d.   is unlike consumer installment debt in that the borrower pledges real property if the terms of the loan are not fulfilled.

    e.   *a* and *c* are both correct.

3. An over-the-counter market
   a. is a retail market.
   b. relies on the open-outcry method.
   c. limits the number of traders.
   d. specializes in variegated assets.
   e. usually precedes an auction market.

4. The market with the largest daily volume is the
   a. U.S. stock market.
   b. foreign-exchange market.
   c. U.S. bond market.
   d. Euro-bond market.
   e. U.S. real estate market.

5. Most trades in the foreign-exchange market
   a. are open outcry.
   b. are conducted to finance trade.
   c. are conducted to finance international investment.
   d. reflect speculation by banks about currency movements.
   e. are swaps.

C 6. If you want to gamble on your belief that the value of the pound is about to fall more than the rest of the market expects, but you want to limit your potential losses, you could
   a. buy pounds forward.
   b. sell pounds forward.
   c. buy a put option on pounds.
   d. buy a call option on pounds.
   e. buy pounds spot.

7. Foreign-exchange futures
   a. account for a larger volume than the forward market.
   b. typically have a value of $50,000.
   c. are generally traded between banks.
   d. are tailor-made for each buyer or seller.
   e. typically trade in $1 million increments.

8. U.S. government securities
   a. are traded in an over-the-counter market.
   b. require all dealers to maintain a deposit.
   c. are typically purchased by corporations.
   d. have no market risk.
   e. are sought after because of the high interest rate paid.

9. Owners of government securities who are worried that interest rates may rise and that the value of the security may fall can buy the right to sell the security at a striking price. That is, they can
   a. buy a put option.
   b. sell a put option.
   c. buy a call option.
   d. sell a call option.

10. The key feature of state and local government bonds is
    a. that they have no market risk.
    b. that the interest earned is not subject to federal income tax.
    c. the liquidity offered by auction-market trading.
    d. that they effectively subsidize the federal government.
    e. their attractiveness to foreign investors.

11. Which of the following assets is sold in a retail market?
    a. foreign currency
    b. U.S. government bonds
    c. futures contracts
    d. corporate stock
    e. real estate

Topics for Discussion

1. Program trading, particularly in stock index futures, has come in for much criticism lately. Program trading is simply programming a computer to compare the price of a stock index future, near maturity, with the value of the underlying stocks. If the price of the index is higher than the cost of acquiring the underlying stocks, the computer sells the index and buys the underlying stocks. In futures markets it is never necessary to own in order to sell. The future sale obligates you to provide a specified bundle of stocks at a specific date, which the purchase of those stocks today, at a lower price, will allow you to do. Of course, you could sell the index now and gamble that you will be able to buy the stocks later for less. Given the large number of stocks in an index, both speculating and arbitrage are greatly facilitated by computers. Is this good or bad?

2. The text points out that owners of exchanges try to find new and better contract forms to increase business. Do you think that the self-interest of owners of exchanges and owners of seats at exchanges always drives them to serve the public interest? Does the invisible hand always work here?

Exercise Questions

1. Assume you own $1 million in government securities and a put option with a strike price of $950,000 and a premium of $10,000. (The premium is the price of the option.)

   a. If interest rates fall next week, would you exercise the option?

   b. How far must the value of your securities fall before you would consider exercising the option?

   c. Calculate your losses if the value of the securities falls to $900,000 before you exercise the option.

   d. Calculate your profit if the value of the securities rises to $1,050,000.

2. An importer owes 1 million yen in 90 days. Describe the potential risk and reward of the following options:

   a. Do nothing. Buy yen spot in 90 days.

   b. Buy yen today. Place them in a Euroyen account and earn interest.

   c. Keep your dollars earning interest here. Buy yen forward.

   d. Buy a call option on yen.

3. Match the asset market with its identifying feature.

   1. Interest income on these bonds is not subject to federal income tax.

   2. These securities are sold in auction markets and over the counter, but 90 percent of the total trading occurs at the New York Stock exchange.

   3. Banks hold these securities because they wish to hold low-risk assets.

   4. The borrower pledges real property if the terms of the loan are not fulfilled.

   5. This market is the largest market in the world in terms of the volume of daily trading.

   6. These securities always trade at face value; they are perfectly liquid.

   7. The returns available on these bonds are higher than those available on U.S. government bonds and are subject to federal income taxes.

   a. bank deposits

   b. foreign-exchange market

    c. U.S. government securities market

    d. state and local government bonds

    e. corporate bond market

    f. corporate stock market

    g. mortgage and consumer debt markets

4.   The dollar continued its surprising surge, driven by near-panic buying as traders rushed to cover bets that the dollar would continue to decline. . . .
Traders said buying turned furious as the dollar climbed above key points on technical charts that many traders use to predict currency movements. The move, in turn, triggered automatic orders that customers left with banks to buy dollars at predetermined levels. The rush to buy dollars resulted in a so-called squeeze that sent traders who had bet on a dollar decline to cover their losses. *Wall Street Journal,* May 12, 1995, p. C1.

This trading most likely occured in an (auction/over-the-counter) market.

Answers to Self-Tests

Completion

1.	auction	8.	forward
2.	wholesale	9.	pays, strike price
3.	put	10.	financial, real
4.	Euro-	11.	liabilities
5.	floaters	12.	two
6.	general obligation, revenue	13.	yield
7.	derivatives		

True-False

1.	False	7.	True
2.	False	8.	False
3.	True	9.	True
4.	True	10.	False
5.	False	11.	True
6.	False		

Multiple Choice

1.	e	7.	b
2.	b	8.	a
3.	e	9.	a
4.	b	10.	b
5.	d	11.	e
6.	c		

Answers to Exercise Questions

1. *a.* No. Lower interest rates imply higher security prices, so the option to sell at a low price is unattractive.
    b. To $950,000.
    c. $60,000. This is composed of the capital loss of $50,000, as the security once worth $1 million is sold for $950,000, plus the $10,000 premium. Note that without the option the loss would have been $100,000.
    d. $40,000. This is the capital gain less the premium paid on the unexercised option.

2. *a.* The value of the yen could rise or fall while you do nothing. If it rises, you will be forced to pay more dollars for the goods ordered. If it falls, you will pay fewer dollars. Unless you are good at predicting changes in the exchange rate, this is not a good option.
    b, c. Both options achieve the same thing—they earn interest and avoid exchange-rate risk. Because of a kind of arbitrage that will be discussed in a later chapter, the two options should pay nearly the same amount.
    d. A call option protects against a rise in the value of the yen, since you can buy the yen at an agreed-on striking price. But, should the yen fall, you can still profit by not exercising the option and paying less. Of course, either way you owe a premium. The added flexibility may or may not be worth the premium.

3.
1.	d	5.	b
2.	f	6.	a
3.	c	7.	e
4.	g		

4. over-the-counter

CHAPTER 5   Interest Rates

Learning Objectives

1. Explain what interest rates are, and calculate present values, future values, and interest rates.

2. Distinguish between the real rate of interest and the nominal rate of interest.

3. List the seven factors that affect interest rates, and explain their effects.

4. Draw a yield curve and explain the factors that determine its slope.

Key Terms, Concepts, and Institutions

interest rate
present value
future value
compound interest
present discounted value
liquidity
information costs
tax attribute
term structure of interest rates
nominal interest rate
preferred habitat theory
marginal tax rate

default-sensitivity attribute
junk bonds
venue, or political attribute
currency attribute
maturity attribute
yield curve
liquidity premium
prime commercial loan rate
risk premium
seasoned
real interest rate
pure rate of interest

Self-Test: Completion

1. The interest rate relates _____ values and _____ values.

2. The higher the interest rate, the _____ the present value of a future value for a specified date.

3. The less liquid the security, the _____ the interest rate the borrower must pay to sell the security to an investor.

4. The interest rates on securities believed to be more sensitive to default risk are (higher/the same as/lower) than those on securities less sensitive to default risk.

5. Interest rates on offshore dollar bonds are usually (higher/the same as/lower) than those on domestic dollar bonds.

6. If Standard & Poor's lowered its rating on a company's debt from single A to triple B, the interest rates that the company would have to offer to attract investors would probably (increase/not change/decrease).

7. If the dollar is depreciating at 4 percent a year compared to the Japanese yen and if unrestricted Japanese securities pay 6 percent a year, then comparable U.S. securities would have to pay about

    _____ percent to compete.

8. If anticipated inflation is 8 percent, the nominal interest rate is 12 percent, and the tax rate is 50 percent, then the real after-tax rate of

    interest is _____ percent.

9. If interest rates rise, bond prices (rise/fall).

10. The interest rate that banks charge on loans to their best commercial

    customers is called the _____ rate.

Self-Test: True-False

1. The more liquid the market, the lower the transactions costs.

2. The interest income of federal government securities is not subject to state income taxes.

3. Increases in the highest marginal tax rates lead to a decrease in the spread between the interest rates on taxable securities and nontaxable securities.

4. An investor in the 28 percent marginal tax bracket would be indifferent between a taxable security with a 14 percent interest rate and a nontaxable security with a 10 percent interest rate.

5. Usually the interest rates on long-term securities are higher than those on short-term securities.

6. As the anticipated inflation rate increases, bond prices decrease.

7. As inflation increases, interest rates on long-term securities usually fall relative to interest rates on short-term securities.

8. Increases in the supply of nontaxable securities lead to a decline in the differential between the interest rates on taxable securities and the interest rates on nontaxable securities.

9. As interest rates fall in general, interest rates on taxable securities rise relative to interest rates on nontaxable securities.

10. The differential between interest rates on U.S. government bonds and interest rates on corporate bonds increases during recessions, due to the higher probability of default on corporate bonds.

Self-Test: Multiple Choice

1. Rank the following assets according to their degree of liquidity
    a. residential real estate
    b. U.S. Treasury bills
    c. corporate bonds
    d. U.S. government agency bonds

2. What is the present value of a bond that promises to pay $2,500 in two years if the discount rate of interest is 15 percent?
    a. $1,890.36
    b. $2,173.91
    c. $2,875.00
    d. $3,306.25
    e. none of the above

3. Junk bonds
    a. are unrated bonds or bonds issued by firms that previously have not issued bonds.
    b. usually offer a higher rate of interest than conventional bonds.
    c. are bonds on which the issuer has defaulted.
    d. are considered more risky than conventional bonds.
    e. are all but c.

4. Interest rates on securities issued by U.S. government agencies are higher than U.S. Treasury issues with the same maturity due to the
    a. liquidity attribute.
    b. tax attribute.
    c. inflation attribute.
    d. political attribute.
    e. currency attribute.

5. All the following are managed interest rates *except* the
   a. prime rate.
   b. discount rate.
   c. rates on AAA corporate bonds.
   d. rates on certificates of deposit.
   e. rates on U.S. Treasury savings bonds.

6. All the following features are associated with liquid markets *except*
   a. lower interest rates, compared to illiquid assets.
   b. low transactions costs.
   c. that the amount of the security outstanding is small.
   d. that the security has been traded extensively.
   e. none of the above; all are characteristics of a liquid market.

7. If you put $150 in the bank today, how much will you have in five years if the relevant interest rate is 5.65 percent?
   a. $197.44
   b. $1,408.20
   c. $15.98
   d. $899.81
   e. $158.48

8. How much money must you put in the bank today in order to receive $5,000 at the end of four years if the relevant interest rate is 5 percent?
   a. $1,250
   b. $4,113.51
   c. $4,761.90
   d. none of the above

9. Interest rates on high-grade corporate bonds are higher than the rates on U.S. Treasury bills partly due to
   a. the tax attribute.
   b. the default-sensitivity attribute.
   c. the political attribute.
   d. the maturity attribute.
   e. b and d.

Topics for Discussion

1. Why do yield curves typically have a positive slope?

2. The May 15, 1995, issue of the *Wall Street Journal* reported that Brandon Brown, head of research at Mitsubishi Finance International, Ltd., in London stated that investors are not likely to change their assessment of the dollar's price in the near future, but that a

reassessment would come if the Federal Reserve were to raise interest rates. Would the dollar rise or fall against the yen if the Fed were to raise interest rates? Why?

3. Suppose that you anticipate that the rate of inflation will increase to 10 percent this year. Would you rather be a lender holding a $5,000 bond that pays a fixed 8 percent interest or the borrower who issued the bond? Defend your answer.

4. What is meant by the tax attribute?

5. Why are securities of U.S. government agencies considered more sensitive to default risk than U.S. Treasury securities?

Exercise Questions

1. List the seven factors that affect the interest rates on securities .

2. The May 15, 1995, issue of the *Wall Street Journal*, p. C19, reported that the Treasury's 30-year bond yielded 6.99 percent, while the latest Treasury 10-year notes yielded 6.67 percent. Two-year notes yielded 6.17 percent, while 6-month Treasury bills yielded 5.65 percent. Complete Table 5.1.

Table 5.1 Yield to Maturity for Selected Securities

Type of security	Years to maturity (maturity date – 1995)	Yield to maturity (percent)
Treasury bonds, due 2025		
Treasury notes, due 2005		
Treasury notes, due 1997		
Treasury bills, 6 months		

Using your answers from Table 5.1, draw a yield curve in Figure 5.1.

Figure 5.1 A Yield Curve

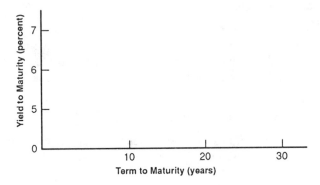

The yield curve slopes (up/down).

3. Figure 5.2 depicts the market for commercial paper. Suppose that Treasury-bill yields increase in anticipation of the Fed's tightening up credit. Show on the graph what will happen in the market for commercial paper.

Figure 5.2 The Market for Commercial Paper

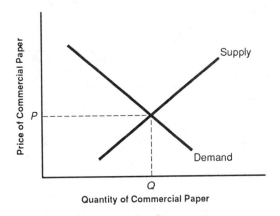

The price of commercial paper will (rise/fall).

The yield on commercial paper will (rise/fall).

4. If you put $500 in the bank today at an interest rate of 8 percent, how much money will you have after 3 years?

5. Tina Nohr is an investor in a 34 percent tax bracket and is trying to decide whether to buy a Florida Board of Education bond yielding 7.25 percent or a J. C. Penney Company bond with similar characteristics yielding 9.8 percent. All other things being equal, which bond should Tina buy? Defend your answer.

6. Ever since Orange County declared bankruptcy in December after suffering $1.7 billion in investment losses in its main investment fund, officials there have been looking for creative ways to meet their debt obligations. Unfortunately, some of the solutions that have been proposed are wholly unacceptable to bond holders. . . . If Orange County does not honor the letter of its debt obligations, it could have a negative effect on the ratings of short-term debt across the state, say market analysts. . .

   Among the biggest buyers of California's short-term debt are money-market funds, which are prohibited from owning anything but the highest-rated debt, says Blake Anderson, director of municipal research at Putnam. . . . "If they're not rated as investment grade, a prudent and conservatively mangaged fund ought not to include those bonds in a fund that's supposed to have an almost riskless character," he says. *Wall Street Journal*, May 18, 1995, p. C21.

   a. Who will be rating the short-term debt of the state?

   b. What ratings are investment grade?

   c. If the short-term debt is not rated as investment grade, what will happen to the interest rate on new issues of California's short term debt?

   d. What will happen to the price of existing short-term debt?

7. Select the correct terms for this January 1, 1995, article from the *Wall Street Journal*, p. A6.

   Standard & Poor's Corp. (raised/lowered) its debt ratings on Chrysler Corp. and Ford Motor Co., saying the carmakers already have amassed enough cash to weather the next recession. . . . The (improved/lower) ratings for Chrysler and Ford, which had been expected, should help the auto makers to (raise/lower) their borrowing costs. . . . The revised ratings also helped (boost/lower) prices of some debt issues of the carmakers and their credit subsidiaries.

Answers to Self-Tests

Completion

1.	present, future	6.	increase
2.	lower	7.	10
3.	higher	8.	−2
4.	higher	9.	fall
5.	higher	10.	prime commercial loan rate

True-False

1.	True	5.	True
2.	False	6.	True
3.	False	7.	False
4.	False (After taxes, the investor would get 10.08 percent on the taxable security.)	8.	True
		9.	False
		10.	True

Multiple Choice

1.	b, d, c, a (in order of decreasing liquidity)	5.	c
		6.	c
2.	a	7.	a
3.	e	8.	b
4.	a	9.	e

Answers to Exercise Questions

1. liquidity
   information costs
   tax attribute
   default-sensitivity attribute
   political attribute
   currency attribute
   term structure (maturity)

2.

Answer to Table 5.1 Yield to Maturity for Selected Securities

Type of security	Years to maturity (maturity date – 1995)	Yield to maturity (percent)
Treasury bonds, due 2025	30	6.99
Treasury notes, due 2005	10	6.67
Treasury notes, due 1997	2	6.17
Treasury bills, 6 months	$1/2$	5.65

Answer to Figure 5.1 A Yield Curve

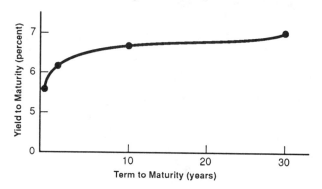

The yield curve slopes up.

3. **Answer to Figure 5.2** The Market for Commercial Paper

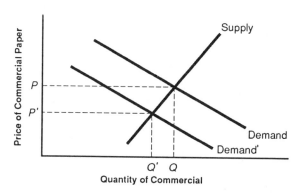

fall; rise

4. $FV = PV(1 + r)^n = 500(1 + .08)^3 = \$629.86$.

5. The Florida Board of Education bond is not subject to federal income taxes, so its after-tax yield is 7.25 percent. If Tina is in a 34 percent tax bracket, she will get to keep 66 percent of the yield of the J. C. Penney bond, or 6.468 percent. All other things being equal, Tina should buy the Florida Board of Education bond.

6.   *a.* Moody's and Standard & Poor's
   - *b.* For Moody's, investment grades are Aaa, Aa, A, and Baa. For Standard & Poor's, investment grades are AAA, AA, A, and BBB.
   - *c.* It will increase to compensate investors for the increased risk of default.
   - *d.* The price will decrease so that investors receive a higher yield to compensate for the additional risk.

7. raised; improved, lower; boost

CHAPTER 6   The Depository Institutions Industry

Learning Objectives

1. Understand the evolution from state banking to national banking to the Federal Reserve System.

2. Explain the rules governing branch banking, interstate banking, and capital-asset ratios.

3. Describe the impact of rules governing branch banking, interstate banking, and capital-asset ratios.

4. Appreciate the roles the FDIC, the Fed, and the Comptroller of the Currency currently play in regulating and serving the banking industry.

5. Contrast the asset and liability composition of the major depository institutions and understand why they are composed differently.

Key Terms, Concepts, and Institutions

bank notes	correspondent banking
state bank	bank concentration
central bank	economies of scale
national bank	interstate banking
charter	branch banking
Comptroller of the Currency	redlining
Federal Reserve System	depository institution
FDIC	stockholders' equity
capital-asset ratio	wire transfers
CAMEL ratings	maturity matching
thrifts	credit unions
savings banks	deposit assumption
savings and loans	

Self-Test: Completion

1. If larger banks earned a higher rate of return than smaller banks, this would be evidence of _____ in banking.

2. The period of state banking ended in 1863 with the creation of _____ .

3. The practice of refusing to lend within a geographical area, perhaps an inner city, is called _____ . The practice is prohibited under the _____ Act.

4. The FDIC, while it can close a failing bank, is more likely to use _____ .

5. Under the Federal Reserve System, reserves are held either in the bank's own vault as cash or at the _____ .

6. A small bank that maintains deposits at a large bank in return for advice, access to national money markets, and loan participation arrangements is called a _____ .

7. Laws that set ceilings on interest rates on loans are called _____ laws.

8. Banks within a single city use a _____ to net out checks written against each other.

9. In banking, "capital" refers to _____ .

10. Bank capital requirements demand a capital/asset ratio of _____ percent, but give safer assets a lower weight. Cash and short-term government securities have a _____ percent weight, while mortgage loans and business loans have a _____ percent weight.

11. While Congress eliminated most branching restrictions on national banks as of 1997, it also provided that no bank have more than _____ percent of deposits in one state or _____ percent of deposits nationally.

Self-Test: True-False

1. A bank with a 100 percent capital-asset ratio could not make loans.

2. Banks are chartered in order to increase competition.

3. Nationally, the top five banks control more than half the deposits.

4. The distinction between being a member of the Fed or not is fading.

5. The FDIC generally closes failed banks.

6. Correspondence banking allows banks to participate in loans made in other states.

7. The Federal Home Loan Banks supervise all savings and loan associations.

8. An increase in interest rates can make savings and loan associations unprofitable.

9. CAMEL refers to capital adequacy, management, earnings, and liquidity.

10. Banks make mostly home loans, while thrifts focus on business loans.

11. Capital is a specific asset that the bank owns.

12. Savings and loans have received deposit insurance at rates set below the market value.

Self-Test: Multiple Choice

1. One of the problems with the national banking system was
   a. inadequate check-clearing.
   b. rapid fluctuations in the money supply.
   c. charters issued capriciously by the state legislatures.
   d. lack of a uniform bank note.
   e. during a crisis reserves flowed from small to large banks.

2. The Federal Reserve System
   a. allowed banks to maintain reserves at big city banks.
   b. monopolizes the check-clearing business.
   c. allows institutions with reserves at the Fed to borrow from the Fed.
   d. consists of all state and national banks.
   e. has been able to prevent depressions and massive bank failures.

3. To some degree we already have interstate banking because of all the following *except*:
   a. Small firms readily obtain loans nationwide.
   b. Banks can make loans nationwide; only deposit collection is restricted to the home state.
   c. Regulators have allowed some interstate mergers.
   d. Correspondence networks can be nationwide.
   e. Reciprocity compacts exist.

4. The $100,000 ceiling on deposit insurance exists because
   a. even this limited level of insurance significantly reduces bank profits.
   b. people with more money are smarter and will not need the insurance.
   c. private insurance is widespread for the larger deposits.
   d. it was established when few deposits were over $100,000 and has not been changed.
   e. the FDIC hopes the larger depositors will monitor the bank's safety and pressure banks to be safe.

5. A higher capital-asset ratio increases bank safety because
   a. with more capital a bank run is less likely to exhaust reserves.
   b. the bigger the stockholders' share, the larger percentage loss a bank can sustain before depositors' funds are jeopardized.
   c. more capital allows a bank flexibility in pursuing opportunities for profit as they arise.
   d. more capital means the bank has more buildings and equipment which could be sold in desperate times.
   e. all but *d*.

6. Banks are likely to choose a capital-asset ratio that is too low from a social point of view because they are _____ interested in their own rate of return and _____ interested in safety than the public.
   a. more, more
   b. more, less
   c. less, more
   d. less, less
   e. equally, less

7. Concentration in banking
   a. has been declining recently as banks have been broken up.
   b. is more likely to inconvenience depositors than borrowers.

    c.   has permitted large reductions in operating costs and therefore threatens the continued existence of small banks.

    d.   increased substantially as some of the largest banks in a single region have been allowed to merge.

    e.   is likely to decline in the future.

8. Savings and loan associations

    a.   are examined by the Federal Reserve system.

    b.   were encouraged by the government to offer long-term fixed-rate home loans and thus spur home ownership.

    c.   offer mostly short-term commercial and industrial loans.

    d.   began as a device for high income families to avoid taxes.

    e.   that are owned by the depositors account for the majority of the assets held by savings and loans.

9. Until 1863, all the following were true of U.S. banks *except* that

    a.   banks were regulated by the individual states.

    b.   bank notes all had the same value.

    c.   nearly 40 percent of banks failed in their first ten years of operation.

    d.   these failures were largely due to the decline in the value of state bonds held by the banks.

    e.   when a bank failed, depositors usually received a large proportion of the money owed them.

10. The national currency act of 1863

    a.   required banks to deposit 9 dollars of government bonds with the comptroller for every 10 dollars of bank notes issued.

    b.   created a central bank that could adjust the money supply.

    c.   created a variety of currencies.

    d.   created clearinghouse certificates.

    e.   allowed banks to hold reserves in the form of either vault cash or deposits at banks in larger cities.

11. The United States has many more banks than Canada or England because

    a.   the U.S. population is higher.

    b.   more banks provide a greater variety of services.

    c.   more banks creates a safer system.

    d.   there is a populist tendency to distrust the power of large banks.

    e.   the diversity in loan markets requires decentralized institutions.

12. If banks are obligated to pursue social goals such as preferential lending in poor neighborhoods, then

    a.   the cost of providing deposit insurance is likely to fall.

b.   money-market funds may tend to grow slower than banks.
c.   growth in the poor neighborhood will decline.
d.   indirect subsidies of banks can be reduced.
e.   other programs to help poor neighborhoods could be reduced. (Could be good or bad depending on cost effectiveness of alternate programs.)

13.   According to the appendix,
a.   The largest banks tend to be German.
b.   German banks often vote the stock held by their depositors, giving banks about 40 percent of the vote in corporate elections.
c.   English banks are bound more by rules than tradition.
d.   Despite NAFTA, U.S. and Canadian banks do not have the same status in each other's country.
e.   The European Community has created a new regulatory body that will serve as the lender of last resort for all the banks throughout Europe.

Topics for Discussion

1.   How did the Federal Reserve Act of 1913 solve problems of previous systems?

2.   Why were the charters of the first two central banks of the United States allowed to expire?

3.   Describe some limitations to the powers of regulators and examiners.

4.   Describe how bank competition and failure can be beneficial.

5.   Why doesn't the FDIC insure all depositors?

6.   Why do we insure depositors at all? Why can't we rely on depositors to discipline unsafe banks by withdrawing their funds?

7.   Argue for or against the proposal that banks should be able to buy a lower capital-asset ratio by paying a higher insurance rate.

8.   The best way to encourage business development in poor areas is to force banks to make loans on preferential terms.

Exercise Questions

1.   Currently, the Bank of Growth has assets totaling $.5 billion and stockholders' equity of $30 million. The capital/asset ratio is

(*a:* _6_) percent. Since $30 million in assets was raised from stockholders, the other $470 million must represent the depositors' contributions. The rate paid depositors averages 7 percent, and the earnings from assets average 8 percent. So the bank earns

(*b:* _$40_) million from their assets in a given year. In the same year they owe depositors (*c:* _$32.9_) million, which leaves them earnings before operating expenses of (*d:* _$7.1_) million.

If operating expenses are $2 million, then (*e:* _$5.1_) million is left to distribute to stockholders who receive a

(*f:* _17_) percent return.

2. The Bank of Safety also has $.5 billion of assets and operating expenses of $2 million. If $50 million represents the stockholders' equity, then the capital-asset ratio is (*a:* _10%_) percent. The Bank of _$500,000,000_

Safety also earns 8 percent on assets, so they earn (*b:* _40 million_) million just as the Bank of Growth does. There are (*c:* _450,000,000_) million of deposits earning an average of 7 percent, so depositors are owed (*d:* _31,500,000_) in the current year. After operating expenses,

.5 this leaves (*e:* _6,500,000_) million to distribute to stockholders, who 13. receive a (*f:* _13_) percent return.

3. Consider what would happen to these two banks if next year interest rates rose. Depositors would have the option of withdrawing their money and investing it elsewhere. Banks sign loan contracts that typically last a couple of years or more. Therefore, while the banks may be locked into earning 8 percent, depositors could demand 9 percent.

The Bank of Growth still earns (*a:* _40_) million but now owes depositors (*b:* _45_) million. After operating expenses of $2 million, there is a deficit of (*c:* _−7 mill_) million, which must be taken from stockholders' equity. The stockholders' rate of return is a negative (*d:* _14%_) percent.

4. The Bank of Safety faces the same situation. Depositors earn 9 percent, assets 8 percent. Earnings total (*a:* _____) million as before.

Depositors must be paid (*b:* _____) million. After operating

expenses of $2 million, a deficit of (*c:* _____) million remains, which must be taken from stockholders' equity. The return to stockholders is a negative (*d:* _____) percent.

Answers to Self-Tests

Completion

1.	economies of scale	6.	country correspondent
2.	the National Banking System	7.	usury
3.	redlining, Community	8.	clearinghouse
	Reinvestment	9.	stockholders' equity
4.	deposit assumption	10.	8, 0, 100
5.	Fed	11.	30, 10

True-False

1.	False	7.	False
2.	False	8.	True
3.	False	9.	True
4.	True	10.	False
5.	False	11.	False
6.	True	12.	True

Multiple Choice

1.	a	8.	b
2.	c	9.	b
3.	a	10.	e
4.	e	11.	d
5.	b	12.	e
6.	b	13.	b
7.	d		

Answers to Exercise Questions

1.	*a.*	6	2.	*a.*	10
	b.	$40		*b.*	$40
	c.	$32.9		*c.*	$450
	d.	$7.1		*d.*	$31.5
	e.	$5.1		*e.*	$6.5
	f.	17		*f.*	13

3. *a.* $40
    b. $42.3
    c. $4.3
    d. 14¹/₃

4. *a.* $40
    b. $40.5
    c. $2.5
    d. 5

CHAPTER 7   Inside the Depository Institution

Learning Objectives

1. Describe the bank's balance sheet, define each item, and determine whether it is an asset or a liability.

2. Show which assets are considered primary and which secondary reserves.

3. Understand how compensating balances raise the effective interest rate for a borrower.

4. Distinguish between asset management and liability management.

5. Explain the risk a bank takes if the maturities of its assets and liabilities are seriously mismatched.

6. Explain the different types of business loans.

7. List ten financial services for which banks receive fees, and explain the risks associated with some of these activities.

8. Explain the risks and rewards banks face by speculating in the foreign-exchange and money markets.

Key Terms, Concepts, and Institutions

letter of credit
checkable deposits
demand deposits
other checkable deposits
implicit interest
liability
asset
collateral
revolving credit

secondary reserves
commercial paper
call loans
credit rationing
customer relationship
term loans
line of credit
compensating (or supporting)
    balances

58

time deposits
passbook savings account
nonnegotiable certificate of
    deposit
negotiable certificate of deposit
amortize
federal funds
banker's acceptance
trade acceptance
earning assets
primary reserves
explicit interest
off-balance-sheet
    financing
business loans
foreign loans
consumer loans
home-equity loans
standby letter of credit
vault cash
credit card loans

large CDs
prime rate
trade acceptance
cash items in the process of
    collection
transactions deposits
asset management
liability management
repurchase agreements (RPs, repos)
Eurodollar
LIBOR
mortgage loan
real estate loans
interest-rate swaps
trust departments
savings deposits
federal-funds rate
capital account
interest-rate risk
payment or settlement risk
liquidity risk

Self-Test: Completion

1. A large proportion of a bank's liabilities are _____ term, while
    most of their assets are _____ term.

2. Banks pay _____ interest on demand deposits by providing free
    services.

3. A letter of credit is an example of _____ , where a bank earns
    fees by assuming risks that do not show up on its balance sheet.

4. Most consumer loans are made for the purchase of _____ .

5. Usually, long-term interest rates are (higher/lower) than short-term
    rates.

6. If banks expect interest rates to rise, they should buy (long-/short-) term
    securities.

7. If a seller draws an order to pay on a buyer's bank, and the order is
    accepted, it is known as a _____ .

8. The larger the loan, the (higher/lower) the interest rate, all other things being equal.

9. _____ are loans made to security dealers and brokers, often on a (renewable) one-day basis.

10. If a bank sold Treasury bills to acquire funds, this action would be characterized as (asset/liability) management.

Self-Test: True-False

1. The federal-funds rate is the rate the Fed charges eligible institutions to borrow from it.

2. A line of credit is an arrangement whereby the bank agrees to make loans up to a certain amount almost on demand.

3. Anyone can buy a negotiable certificate of deposit.

4. The purpose of reserve requirements is to ensure the safety of the depositors' funds.

5. Banks are now permitted to pay corporations explicit interest on their demand accounts.

6. Selling Treasury bills to increase liquidity is an example of liability management.

7. A compensating balance requirement is legally binding on the borrower.

8. A bank needing liquidity might buy federal funds.

9. Cash items in the process of collection are extremely liquid and count as a part of primary reserves.

10. Compensating balances reduce the effective interest cost to the borrower.

11. The prime rate is the highest rate a bank would charge a borrower.

Self-Test: Multiple Choice

1. A bank's primary reserves consist of
   a. demand deposits with other banks.
   b. vault cash.
   c. reserves with the Fed.
   d. all the above.
   e. only b and c.

2. Which of the following would a bank hold as part of secondary reserves?
    a. vault cash
    b. Treasury bills
    c. CIPC
    d. deposits at the Fed
    e. demand deposits

3. If the Treasury-bill rate is less than the federal-funds rate but greater than the rate on negotiable certificates of deposits, then a bank needing funds would be likely to
    a. sell Treasury bills.
    b. borrow federal funds.
    c. buy federal funds.
    d. buy negotiable certificates of deposit.
    e. issue negotiable certificates of deposit.

4. Small banks are likely to use which of the following instruments of liability management?
    a. repurchase agreements
    b. negotiable CDs
    c. Eurodollars
    d. federal funds
    e. commercial paper

5. Which of the following are *not* liquid assets for a bank?
    a. Consumer loans.
    b. Call loans.
    c. Mortgage loans.
    d. None of the above; all are liquid loans.
    e. Only *a* and *b*.

6. Banks perform other services besides taking deposits and making loans. Which of the following activities are banks *not* permitted to undertake?
    a. arranging interest-rate swaps
    b. acting as dealers in the money markets
    c. acting as brokers in the real estate market
    d. administering trusts
    e. acting as dealers in the foreign-exchange market

7. All the following are liabilities of the bank *except*
    a. repurchase agreements.
    b. checkable deposits.
    c. money-market deposit accounts.
    d. bankers' acceptances.
    e. demand deposits at U.S. depository institutions.

8. All the following can be considered part of primary reserves *except*
   a. commercial paper.
   b. vault cash.
   c. deposits at the Fed.
   d. interbank deposits.
   e. none of the above; all of the above can be considered primary reserves.

9. The higher the interest rate charged on loans is,
   a. the smaller the loan is.
   b. the greater the term of the loan.
   c. the more risky the loan is.
   d. the greater the demand for credit.
   e. All the above are correct.

10. If portfolio managers appear to be shortening the maturities of their holdings of international bonds denominated in U.S. dollars, they probably anticipate
    a. a rise in U.S. interest rates.
    b. a fall in U.S. interest rates.
    c. a rise in U.S. bond rates.
    d. *b* and *c*.
    e. *a* and *c*.

Topics for Discussion

1. What prevents a foreign government from declaring its debts null and void?

2. Which assets count as legal reserves for members of the Federal Reserve System?

3. Why do banks have an incentive to reschedule the loan payments of debtor countries that otherwise would default?

4. Suppose you are a real estate developer. Your income is variable, but you have a fixed monthly payroll. Would you prefer to have a term loan or a line of credit? Explain your answer.

5. Would a Treasury bond appear on a bank's books as a loan or a security purchase? How do loans differ from security purchases?

6. WASHINGTON—. . . Comptroller Eugene Ludwig said credit standards have been slipping, and expressed concern that banks, in an attempt to bolster profit, may further relax consumer and business credit as the economy slows. . . . The comptroller's remarks . . . constitute an unusually strong message that regulators will carefully scrutinize national banks'

credit standards and won't tolerate lax loan policies . . . *Wall Street Journal,* April 10, 1995, p. A2.

If the comptroller's regulators do force banks to reduce the volume of risky loans by tightening their loan quality standards, how are banks likely to respond?

Exercise Questions

1. For each of the balance-sheet items in Table 7.1, indicate whether the item is an asset or a liability. If the item is an asset, indicate whether the item may be considered part of primary reserves, secondary reserves, or earning assets.

Table 7.1 Balance-Sheet Exercise

| Item | Asset | | | Liability |
	Primary reserves	Secondary reserves	Earning assets	
Federal funds purchased				
Short-term U.S. government securities				
Money-market accounts				
Federal funds sold				
Banker's acceptances				
Checkable deposits				
Vault cash				
Reserves at the Fed				
Call loans				
Term loans				
Passbook savings accounts				
Real estate loans				
Demand deposits				

2. Suppose the First National Bank of Greentree makes a $150,000 loan to the Mark FitzGerald Landscaping Service at a 12 percent interest rate with a 15 percent minimum compensating balance.

   a. How much of the $150,000 is actually available for Mark FitzGerald to use? $_____ .

    b.   What is the effective rate of interest on this amount? _____
           percent.

    c.   Mr. FitzGerald feels that 12 percent interest is awfully high for his
           loan. What might he do to get First National to offer him a lower rate?

    d.   Suppose Mr. FitzGerald violates his minimum compensating
           balances requirement. What can the bank do?

Crossword Puzzle

ACROSS

3. _____ is considered to be part of a bank's primary reserves.
4. Involve personal relationships with borrowers.
5. Deposits traded among banks and other institutions.
7. _____ bills.
8. This type of loan is often rescheduled if the borrower cannot pay.
10. The rate banks charge their best customers.
11. Business loans with a maturity of one to five years.
13. _____ is the abbreviation for the Keystone State.
14. Banks may not pay interest on _____ deposits.
16. Supporting or _____ balances.
17. _____ reserves include short-term government securities, banker's acceptances, and commercial paper.
18. Dollar-denominated deposits in European and Caribbean banks.
19. The rate at which large international banks lend to each other on the international market (abbr.).

DOWN

1. An arrangement whereby the bank agrees to make loans to a firm up to a certain amount almost on demand.
2. _____ market account.
6. Banker's _____ .
9. Checks that have just been deposited but have not yet been cleared (abbr.).
11. Another type of bank activity.
12. A way to pay implicit interest on demand deposits (abbr.).
13. The most familiar type of savings account.
15. Loans to dealers and brokers.
16. Certificates of deposit (abbr.).

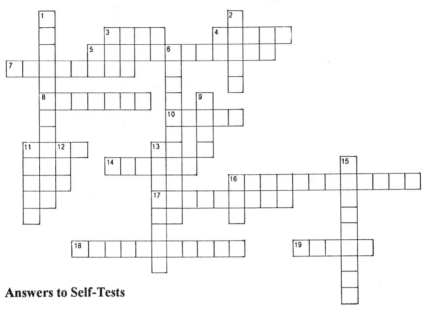

Answers to Self-Tests

Completion

1.	short, long	6.	short
2.	implicit	7.	banker's acceptance
3.	off-balance-sheet financing	8.	lower
4.	durables	9.	call loans
5.	higher	10.	asset

True-False

1.	False	7.	False
2.	True	8.	True
3.	True (If they have the money.)	9.	False
4.	False	10.	False
5.	False	11.	False
6.	False		

Multiple Choice

1.	d	6.	c
2.	b	7.	e
3.	e	8.	a
4.	d	9.	e
5.	c	10.	a

Answers to Exercise Questions

1.
Answer to Table 7.1   Balance-Sheet Exercise

Item	Primary reserves	Secondary reserves	Earning assets	Liability
Federal funds purchased	X			X
Short-term U.S. government securities		X	X	
Money-market accounts				X
Federal funds sold			X	
Banker's acceptances				X
Checkable deposits				X
Vault cash	X			
Reserves at the Fed	X			
Call loans		X	X	
Term loans			X	
Passbook savings accounts				X
Real estate loans			X	
Demand deposits				X

(Asset columns: Primary reserves, Secondary reserves, Earning assets)

2. *a.* $127,500.
   b. 14.12 percent. Mr. FitzGerald must pay 12 percent of $150,000, or $18,000, in interest. Since he can only use $127,500, the effective rate of interest is $18,000/$127,500 = 14.12 percent.
   c. He could offer to provide collateral, and so make the loan less risky for the bank.
   d. Nothing legally, but the bank may refuse him further loans or charge him a higher interest rate on future loans.

Answer to Crossword Puzzle

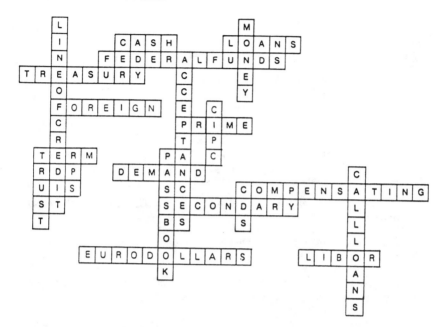

CHAPTER 8   International Banking

Learning Objectives

1. Describe the offshore banking market.

2. List three reasons for the offshore expansion of U.S. banks in the 1960s and 1970s.

3. List four reasons for the expansion of foreign banks in the United States in the 1970s.

4. Explain the concepts of reciprocity and national treatment pertaining to the regulation of foreign banks in the United States.

5. Explain how the growth of international banking has reduced the scope of independent national policies.

Key Terms, Concepts, and Institutions

offshore banking market
reciprocity
national treatment
Eurodollar

Euromark
monetary haven
International Banking Act

Self-Test: Completion

1. _____ are dollar-denominated deposits issued by banks outside the United States.

2. If U.S. law treated foreign banks just as the foreign country treated U.S. banks, then it would be following the principle of _____ .

3. Monetary havens are places where offshore banks _____ .

4. Those branches of foreign banks that sell deposits to U.S. residents are required to _____ .

5. Does the United States follow the principle of reciprocity or national treatment? _____

6. The number of domestic banks in European countries is typically _____ than the number in the United States.

7. Interest rates on offshore deposits _____ the interest rates on comparable domestic deposits.

8. The _____ established the principle of national treatment.

9. U.S. bank expansion abroad was most rapid in the _____ , while foreign bank expansion in the United States was most rapid in the

_____ .

Self-Test: True-False

1. The principle motivation for dollar deposits outside the United States is to avoid U.S. regulation.

2. The IBA slowed the growth of foreign banks in the United States.

3. Offshore banks are required to hold reserves at the Fed against their dollar-denominated deposits.

4. U.S. banks operating in Europe would turn to the Fed should a run in Europe develop.

5. U.S. banks established foreign facilities in part to serve their U.S. corporate loan clients that were expanding abroad.

6. Mexico is a monetary haven.

7. Foreign banks operating in the United States are regulated as if they were U.S. banks.

8. It is quite difficult for countries to set independent reserve requirements since differences in requirements cause banks to shift deposits between countries.

9. Foreign banks operating in the United States must join the Federal Reserve and hold reserves there.

10. Offshore deposits tend to pay higher interest rates partly because offshore banks incur lower costs than domestic banks.

11. Income of foreign branches is taxed only when the profits are repatriated.

Self-Test: Multiple Choice

1. A U.S. parent bank with a foreign subsidiary
   a. pays income tax on the subsidiary's earnings whether they are transferred to the parent or not.
   b. could conceivably survive even if the subsidiary failed.
   c. is sometimes required to have partial foreign ownership.
   d. faces the same tax treatment as a foreign branch.
   e. both b and c.

2. U.S. banks set up foreign offices at an accelerated pace in the 1960s
   a. to separate themselves from U.S. firms.
   b. to get access to less-restrictive rules that allowed foreign competitors to offer higher interest rates and still turn a profit.
   c. because the U.S. was growing only slowly.
   d. because foreign banks were weak and the markets ripe for takeover.
   e. all the above.

3. Foreign banks expanded rapidly in the United States in the 1970s to
   a. avoid regulations in the home country.
   b. help finance expanding world trade.
   c. serve ethnic markets.
   d. get better access to dollar deposits.
   e. all the above.

4. The International Banking Act of 1978 (IBA)
   a. required the United States to treat foreign banks however foreign governments treated U.S. banks.
   b. required the United States to treat foreign banks, in large measure, as if they were U.S. banks.
   c. did not require even large foreign banks to hold reserves at the Fed.

    d.   will accelerate the expansion of foreign banks.

    e.   reduced the effectiveness of monetary control.

5.   Which of the following statements is false?

    a.   Interest rates on offshore deposits are greater than interest rates on comparable domestic deposits.

    b.   Offshore banks are virtually unregulated by the countries in which they are located.

    c.   Depositors shift funds to banks located in monetary havens to take advantage of lower tax rates.

    d.   Most of the foreign offices of U.S. banks are branches.

    e.   A branch bank cannot fail while its parent remains open for business.

6.   U.S. banks expanded abroad to

    a.   avoid interest ceilings on deposits.

    b.   follow the foreign expansion of U.S. firms.

    c.   avoid restrictions on growth.

    d.   set up branches that could avoid taxes.

    e.   all but *d.*

7.   Foreign banks now in the United States are here to

    a.   avoid interest ceilings on deposits.

    b.   provide Americans with other currencies as the use of the dollar declined.

    c.   follow their home-country firms and residents.

    d.   avoid reserve requirements on resident deposits.

    e.   all but *b.*

8.   Foreign-owned banks in the United States must hold reserves at the Fed

    a.   to ensure the safety of the deposits belonging to U.S. residents.

    b.   if their deposits are less than $1 billion.

    c.   in order to enhance the effectiveness of U.S. monetary control.

    d.   only if they are members of the Federal Reserve System.

    e.   only if they hold a federal, as opposed to a state, license.

9.   International banking

    a.   increases competition.

    b.   discourages mergers of banks.

    c.   helps maintain the distinctions between national currencies and regulations.

    d.   helps monetary policy.

    e.   allows banks to dodge regulations and increase their scale; this reduces the cost of some bank functions.

10. The text argues that a chain-reaction collapse of international banks is unlikely because
    a. offshore branches are apt to have the same loan policies as the onshore head office.
    b. offshore branches of U.S. banks are examined by the same agencies that examine the onshore branches.
    c. offshore branches cannot fail independently; solvency is based on the solvency of the head office.
    d. each central bank has agreed to provide the liquidity necessary in its region.
    e. all the above.

Topics for Discussion

1. While currency conversion is possible, currencies retain independent identities because the conversion ratios change widely and unpredictably. Forward markets generally exist for a year or less. Stabilizing currencies would have some advantages, but would remove the last remaining distinctions between currencies. Should currencies be stabilized? Does the European monetary union make sense?

2. The text argues that an international banking collapse is unlikely because U.S. examination extends to offshore branches and because the home office's loan policies generally extend to the branches. This is the same examination that allowed the collapse of Penn Square, Continental Illinois, and many savings and loan associations. How confident are you that U.S. examination could prevent an international banking collapse? Just as Continental Illinois was formally separate from Penn Square, but was in fact closely linked by a common loan pool, banks from different countries routinely swap loans. Is this linkage dangerous or beneficial?

3. Japanese banks dominate the international market. Should we gut our domestic restrictions on branch banking, mergers, and interstate banking in order to allow massive U.S. banks to form that could compete with the Japanese giants?

4. An alternative to preserving separate national currencies and separate national money supplies is to create regional currencies and regulators. Is this the correct approach?

5. The ease of currency conversion and movement raises the question of whether money supply definitions that distinguish between currency or country of origin have any meaning. Do national currencies still exist in a meaningful way?

Answers to Self-Tests

Completion

1. Eurodollars
2. reciprocity
3. incur lower costs
4. be federally insured
5. national treatment

6. smaller
7. exceed
8. International Banking Act
9. 1960s and 1970s, 1970s

True-False

1. True
2. True
3. False
4. False
5. True
6. False

7. True
8. True
9. False
10. True
11. False

Multiple Choice

1. *e*
2. *b*
3. *e*
4. *b*
5. *c*
6. *e*

7. *c*
8. *c*
9. *a* (Competition will force profits to be passed on to customers.)
10. *e*

CHAPTER 9   The Failure of the Deposit-Insurance System

Learning Objectives

1. Explain why the savings and loan industry became such a heavy burden on the taxpayer.

2. Apportion blame for the poor thrift performance between crooks, the U.S. Congress, various administrations, academic economists, the system, and the public.

3. Explain the poor performance of banks in recent years.

4. Discuss institutional reforms to deal with the problems of banks and thrifts.

Key Terms, Concepts, and Institutions

Regulation Q
disintermedition
maturity matching
interest-rate risk
FIRREA
LDC debt
Keating Five

zombie thrifts
Resolution Trust Corporation
Office of Thrift Supervision
Savings Association Insurance Fund
Bank Insurance Fund
creative accounting
deregulation

Self-Test: Completion

1. Thrifts with a negative net worth, but still in operation, are sometimes called _____ .

2. _____ set interest-rate ceilings for thrifts ad banks until

   _____ .

3. Both the _____ and the _____ are now administered
   by the FDIC.

4. The immediate purpose of the FIRREA was to _____ .

5. The single most important step taken by the FIRREA to avoid another
   thrift crisis was to _____ .

6. The principle method of hedging against interest-rate risk is to

   _____ .

7. Losses from the savings and loan crisis are estimated to be about
   $ _____ billion. Of these losses, nearly 40 percent occurred in
   the state of _____ , illustrating that state regulatory policies
   varied widely.

8. The text argues that the number and quality of bank examiners should
   have increased due to the Reagan administration's policy of

   _____ .

9. Crooks accounted for about _____ percent of losses suffered by
   thrifts.

10. The system of long-term loans financed by short-term deposits was
    initiated by the _____ administration.

11. Banks argue that higher deposit-insurance premiums will reduce bank
    profits. This is true only in _____ .

Self-Test: True-False

1. When interest rates rise, banks do less well than thrifts.

2. The FSLIC hid the deteriorating position of the insurance fund from
   Congress and the public.

3. The text argues that crooks were not the lions that killed the thrifts, but
   the jackals that fed off the decaying carcasses.

4. The policy of not recognizing losses as they occurred was a success in the LDC crisis, but a failure in the thrift crisis.

5. Regulation Q discriminated in favor of poor households.

6. The FSLIC had the funds necessary to close insolvent thrifts.

7. Given the failure of the FSLIC, a large number of state-run insurance agencies have developed.

8. Commercial banks are now allowed to buy solvent thrifts and turn them into branches.

9. Deposit insurance discourages risk taking by bank managers.

10. Closing one loophole creates incentives to open others.

11. As savings and loans became insolvent, they reduced operations dramatically.

12. Crooked thrift managers might grant high-interest loans they thought would not be repaid and then book the temporary flow of interest payments as profit.

Self-Test: Multiple Choice

1. Savings and loans became a mecca for crooks because
   a. a small investment brought control of a large volume of deposits.
   b. insurance meant depositors had little incentive to monitor or control crooked behavior.
   c. deregulation made massive fraud possible.
   d. bank examiners were underpaid and overworked.
   e. all the above.

2. The regulatory system is partially to blame for the thrift failure because
   a. managers of insured but insolvent firms had nothing to lose but everything to gain by taking risks.
   b. Regulation Q reduced maturity matching.
   c. long-term deposits and short-term loans set thrifts up to fail.
   d. thrift charters became so expensive that profits were impossible.
   e. the implicit tax on home ownership undermined the thrifts' solvency.

3. Despite flaws in the insurance system, the system seemed to work well for a time until
   a. more bank charters were issued; this reduced the value of a charter.
   b. the later 1970s when oil prices rose.

    c. the early 1980s when LDCs renegotiated debts.

    d. the late 1980s when the recession began and reduced home values.

    e. the early 1960s when interest rates fell.

4. Economists are partially responsible for the thrift failure because

    a. they wanted to subsidize housing without raising taxes.

    b. they failed to recognize that higher interest rates would doom thrifts.

    c. they failed to understand that without Regulation Q high-risk thrifts would be able to bid funds away form low-risk thrifts.

    d. deregulation was not accompanied by enhanced supervision.

    e. they advocated procrastination by the FSLIC.

5. Continental Illinois

    a. relied largely on small-scale deposits.

    b. was a medium-size bank.

    c. failed and only deposits under $100,000 were paid off.

    d. offers an example of deposit assumption.

    e. illustrates that the FDIC responded differently to the failure of large and small institutions.

6. Bank loans to LDCs

    a. never threatened the solvency of our largest institutions.

    b. became burdensome to LDCs when inflation rose rapidly.

    c. allowed OPEC earnings in U.S. banks to be used by LDCs to buy oil.

    d. were resolved through bankruptcy proceedings.

    e. made headlines when Korea defaulted.

7. New regulations include

    a. reduced capital requirements to increase bank profits.

    b. interest payments on reserves held at the Fed.

    c. a series of mandatory "trip wires" so that banks are closed before they become insolvent.

    d. the extension of deposit insurance so that large and small deposits are treated equally.

    e. mandatory long-term loans to problem institutions from the Fed.

8. If a bank's capital falls too low, regulators *must* impose sanctions. Possibilities include

    a. forcing the purchase of additional stock.

    b. raising dividends.

    c. forcing the sale of problem loans.

    d. mandatory layoffs.

    e. forcing out present management.

9. The "let's pretend" policy of the FSLIC included
   a. allowing merged institutions to show a larger net worth than the sum of the two independent institutions' net worth.
   b. forcing savings and loans to record their loans at market value rather than historical value.
   c. allowing thrifts that, by all past definitions, had failed to remain open.
   d. estimating the thrift's income by assuming all loans paid current market rates.
   e. *a* and *c.*

10. While for a time the failure of savings and loans could be blamed on suddenly higher interest rates, lower rates have not ended the failures because
    a. fraud at thrifts has reached epidemic proportions.
    b. the housing market has failed to rebound despite lower interest rates.
    c. loan losses at thrifts have been higher, perhaps due to thrifts embarking on new, unfamiliar businesses.
    d. the failure of some state thrift insurance systems has called the national insurance system into question and depositors demand a higher interest rate to bear the added risk.
    e. the past failures have increased the cost of insurance which is now high enough to be causing some failures.

11. Due to the term characteristics of their assets and liabilities, thrift institutions tend to experience problems when
    a. long-term interest rates rise.
    b. financial intermediation occurs.
    c. the effects of falling interest rates cause withdrawals of deposits from thrifts.
    d. short-term interest rates rise sharply.
    e. none of the above.

12. Regulation Q was supposed to help thrifts by
    a. reducing the interest rate thrifts would have to pay to attract funds.
    b. reducing the flow of funds to thrifts.
    c. giving thrifts the right to offer variable-interest-rate mortgages.
    d. providing thrifts with a secondary mortgage market.
    e. allowing thrifts to enter other businesses.

Topics for Discussion

1. The text argues that the FSLIC was essentially captured by thrifts and failed to exercise oversight. Regulators captured by those they are supposed to regulate is a common problem. The FDIC is now charged with regulating banks and thrifts. Will the FDIC be able to avoid capture? What features of the new regulations appear to be directed at this problem?

2. If deposit insurance is at the heart of the thrift crisis, why not eliminate insurance? If the problem is that people cannot generally evaluate the riskiness of depository institutions, then lack of insurance would provide an incentive for private ratings agencies to develop, similar to Standard & Poor's or Moody's.

3. Procrastination intensified the thrift crisis but helped ameliorate the LDC crisis. Do you think the same tendencies toward procrastination are evident in the debate over the federal budget deficit? Will procrastination help or hurt in this case?

4. The thrift industry owes its existence to the desire to subsidize home ownership. Should home ownership be subsidized? If so, what is the fairest, safest, and most effective method?

5. Now that the regulatory process has been reformed, should we also reform the political process given that crooks and politicians did play a significant role in the crisis? What kinds of reforms would you suggest?

Exercise Questions

1. The purpose of this exercise is to examine the causes of the crisis in savings and loans. You will be given some data, and you will use the material in the chapter to interpret the data. All dollar figures are in billions.[1]

---

[1] All data (except new mortgage rates) are taken from "Insolvency and Risk Taking in the Thrift Industry: Implications for the Future," by James R. Barth, R. Dan Brumbaugh, Daniel Sauerhaft, and George H. K. Wang, in *Contemporary Policy Issues*, 3, no. 5, 1–32. See Tables 2, 3, 5, and 9. The new mortgage rates are from the *Federal Reserve Bulletin*, various issues.

| | Number of thrifts with negative net worth | | Assets of thrifts with net worth < 0 | | Assets of failed |
Year	GAAP*	RAP†	GAAP	RAP	institutions
1980	17	17	$ 0.127	$ 0.127	$ 2.9
1981	65	41	17.3	7.1	15.1
1982	201	80	48.7	13.1	46.8
1983	287	54	78.9	12.6	15.9
1984	434	71	107.3	12.0	9.5

*GAAP refers to generally accepted accounting principles.
†RAP refers to regulatory accounting principles.

    a.   Why are GAAP and RAP different?

    b.   When did the differences appear?

    c.   Have the differences been narrowing or widening?

    d.   "Assets of failed institutions" refers to the assets of the institutions the FSLIC closed or merged. Compare these assets with the assets of thrifts with a GAAP net worth less than 0. How has the policy of FSLIC closings changed?

    e.   How might this policy change affect the behavior of thrifts?

Year	FSLIC reserves (billions)	Cost of solution* (billions)	Cost of assistance undertaken (billions)	New mortgage rates (percent)	Market Value (net worth/ assets) (percent)
1980	$6.5	$ .01	$ .166	12.65%	–12.47%
1981	6.3	1.23	.988	14.74	–17.32
1982	6.3	1.95	1.127	15.12	–12.03
1983	6.4	4.18	.934	12.66	–15.64
1984	5.9	15.77	.849	12.37	– 2.74

*The cost of solution refers to the present-value cost of the least-expensive solution (usually merging) for institutions with negative GAAP net worths. The cost of assistance undertaken is the present-value costs of the new assistance cases undertaken that year. The new mortgage rate is the average effective rate on conventional mortgages on new homes assuming prepayment at the end of 10 years. The market value of net worth/assets is net worth calculated by market value divided by thrift industry assets.

    f.   Why did thrift failures increase just as the rate they earned on new loans increased in 1981 and 1982?

    g.   Despite the drop in interest rates in 1983 and 1984 more thrifts' GAAP net worth became negative. Why?

h. Could the FSLIC have afforded to close all the thrifts with negative GAAP net worths in 1984?

i. Why did the market value of the industry improve so much in 1983 and 1984?

j. How is it possible for more institutions to have negative GAAP net worths at the same time the market value net worth of the industry as a whole is improving?

Answers to Self-Tests

Completion

1. zombies
2. Regulation Q, 1986
3. Savings Association Insurance Find, Bank Insurance Fund
4. close insolvent thrifts
5. raise capital requirements
6. match maturities
7. 100 to 150; Texas
8. deregulation
9. 10 to 20
10. Roosevelt
11. the short run

True-False

1. False
2. True
3. True
4. True
5. False
6. False
7. False
8. True
9. False
10. True
11. False
12. True

Multiple Choice

1. e
2. a
3. a
4. c
5. e
6. c
7. c
8. e
9. e
10. c
11. d
12. a

Answers to Exercise Questions

1.   *a.* GAAP is what accountants were taught to do in school. RAP is an example of a regulator playing "let's pretend."

     b. 1981.

     c. Widening.

     d. It used to be that even some thrifts with positive GAAP net worths were closed or merged. By 1984 only a small fraction of those thrifts with negative GAAP net worths were closed or merged.

     e. Knowing only a small percentage of insolvent thrifts will be closed or merged could encourage risk-taking by thrifts. Those that are insolvent and still operating are literally investing only other people's money.

     f. Higher interest rates hurt thrifts because they specialized in long-term home loans. Their new loans earned the high rates, but the old ones did not. These thrifts had to pay high deposit rates to keep depositors even though the old loans paid lower rates.

     g. The decline in GAAP net worth after 1983 was due to loan losses, not interest-rate risk. Some say the new laws allowing thrifts into previously prohibited businesses led to losses as inexperienced thrifts entered highly competitive markets. Others feel thrifts deliberately took higher risks as the threat of FSLIC closing diminished.

     h. No. The FSLIC would have needed $15 billion and had only about $6 billion.

     i. The decline in interest rates increased the market value of loans.

     j. GAAP net worth carries loans at their historical value, not their market value. A $50,000 loan stays a $50,000 loan regardless of interest-rate changes until fully or partially repaid.

CHAPTER 10　　Some Remaining Issues of Financial Policy

Learning Objectives

1. Discuss the advantages and disadvantages of the proposals to fix the deposit-insurance system.

2. Discuss why the market share of banks is declining and what banks are doing about it.

3. Evaluate the benefits and costs of universal banking.

Key Terms, Concepts, and Institutions

deposit insurance
risk incentive
risk-related insurance premiums
subordinated claim
secondary capital
"too big to fail"
marking to market
insurance ceiling
private insurance

narrow bank
fail-safe bank
book value
commercial banking
investment banking
Glass-Steagall Act
firewall
competition in laxity
universal bank

Self-Test: Completion

1. ＿＿＿＿＿＿ ＿＿＿＿＿＿ ＿＿＿＿＿＿ is measuring a bank's capital at market value rather than book value.

2. A ＿＿＿＿＿＿ claim is a claim that is paid off only after all the claims to which it takes a back seat are paid off.

3. A bank that takes deposits, makes loans, underwrites securities and owns stock is known as _____ .

4. _____ was the policy of extending the FDIC's protection to all depositors of the biggest banks in the country.

5. The _____ the capital-asset ratio, the less incentive a bank has to take excessive risk.

6. It is easy to mark assets to market for which there exist ready markets, but difficult for those assets that are _____ or traded infrequently.

7. Subordinate bonds issued by banks are held by _____ who have little incentive to discipline the bank if it takes excessive risk.

8. _____ banks would issue checkable deposits but would be allowed to own only safe, liquid assets—no commercial loans.

9. The separation of banks and nonbank subsidiaries is called _____ ; the _____ required the separation of commercial and investment banking.

10. One possible solution to the problems of deposit insurance is to force banks to carry their assets on the books at the actual _____ value, rather than at the historical cost of acquisition.

11. The FDIC could (raise/lower) the insurance ceiling to give depositors more incentive to monitor the riskiness of their banks.

12. _____ are firms that help businesses to raise capital by advising them on what stocks and bonds to issue.

Self-Test: True-False

1. Banks have an incentive to prop up weak subsidiaries because the poor performance of a subsidiary reflects badly on the parent.

2. The computer revolution has made banks so much more efficient that the commercial paper market is being replaced by bank loans.

3. The main function of capital is to absorb losses.

4. If banks were obligated to hold more secondary capital, then the market would signal confidence in the bank through the interest rate on bonds.

5. Currently, if interest rates rise and reduce the value of debt instruments, banks must mark down the value of their assets.

6. Equity capital costs less than deposits do.

7. Banks may be broad, rather than narrow, because the loan manager may learn much by keeping an eye on the borrower's deposits.

8. According to the text, the decline in the market share of banks is surprising because as income and wealth rise, it would be natural for people to rely more heavily on banks.

9. An advantage of higher capital-asset ratios is that they make excessive risk-taking a more costly alternative for the insured institution.

10. If a bank fails, depositors bear most of the cost of failure.

11. Making depositors bear some of the costs of bank failures is more likely to hurt large banks than small banks.

Self-Test: Multiple Choice

1. Allowing banks into nonbank businesses would increase the riskiness of banks if
   a. nonbank business earnings and bank earnings were inversely related.
   b. a firewall were successfully constructed.
   c. banks were to make loans to subsidiaries without considering the parental relationship.
   d. insurance providers felt it necessary to bail out subsidiaries as well.
   e. the nonbank businesses were less risky.

2. Marking to market would
   a. mean closing down institutions when the market value of their assets is temporarily less than the market value of their liabilities.
   b. increase the capital of most banks.
   c. be difficult for widely traded bonds.
   d. give less-reliable information to examiners and potential depositors.
   e. allow banks to operate subsidiaries more profitably.

3. The risk that a bank imposes on the FDIC depends on
   a. the riskiness of the bank's individual assets.
   b. the correlation between the risks of the bank's assets.
   c. the maturities of the bank's liabilities.
   d. the quickness with which regulators can determine a bank is unsafe.
   e. all the above.

4. Lower insurance ceilings
   a. would help small banks more than large banks, since small banks tend to have smaller-denomination deposits anyway.
   b. may cause runs, as people hear unsubstantiated rumors of trouble.
   c. have broad support in Washington, D.C.
   d. would eliminate money brokers.
   e. both a and b.

5. Which of the following is *not* a reason for opposing market-value accounting for banks?
   a. Market-value accounting is subjective.
   b. Market-value accounting is inaccurate.
   c. Market-value accounting is costly.
   d. An institution may be shut down just because the value of its assets is temporarily less than the value of its liabilities.
   e. The FDIC's losses in bank failures would be substantially reduced if banks used market-value accounting.

6. Which of the following would result from requiring higher capital-asset ratios for banks?
   a. lower interest rates paid on deposits
   b. more intermediation services from banks
   c. higher interest rates charged on loans
   d. shrinkage of the banking industry
   e. all but b

7. All the following are factors that may limit risk-taking *except*
   a. the memory of the Great Depression.
   b. the efforts of bank examiners.
   c. reluctance on the part of depositors to bear any of the burden of a bank's failure.
   d. the willingness of bank managers to forgo extra earnings in favor of job security.
   e. none of the above; all are factors that inhibit risk-taking.

8. Which of the following is an argument against a minimum capital requirement for depository institutions?
   a. Banks that hold too little capital are, in effect, subsidized by those that hold adequate capital.
   b. Banks that hold too much capital have lower profits than those with adequate capital.
   c. It is difficult for banks to raise capital by selling stock because the price of bank stock is so low.

    d.   Small banks would have an advantage over large banks in raising capital by issuing bonds.

    e.   None of the above.

9.   Which of the following is an argument for lowering the deposit-insurance ceiling?

    a.   Uninsured depositors would be likely to run the bank at the slightest provocation.

    b.   Depositors at large banks would have little incentive to monitor the riskiness of their banks, knowing that the FDIC would not let a large bank fail.

    c.   Uninsured depositors would force risky banks to pay a higher rate of interest on deposits.

    d.   Business depositors always monitor the riskiness of their banks because they hold such large deposits.

    e.   Lowered ceilings would encourage large depositors to take advantage of information on the bank's safety, which is currently readily available.

10.   Firms in industries that banks wish to enter oppose such entry because

    a.   they fear that banks will cut off loans to them in favor of loans to their subsidiaries.

    b.   they fear that banks will have an advantage over them because the banks have special privileges from the government.

    c.   they fear that banks may take on too much risk and fail.

    d.   they argue that banks should not be permitted to engage in outside activities since outside firms are not permitted to engage in banking.

    e.   all the above.

    f.   all except *d.*

11.   The market share of commercial banks has declined; this implies the market share of competitors must have increased. Which competitors increased their market shares?

    a.   only insurance companies

    b.   only thrifts

    c.   pension and trust companies, insurance companies, finance companies, and investment companies

    d.   investment companies and finance companies

    e.   real estate companies

12.   The primary objection to universal banks is that they

    a.   concentrate power.

    b.   are less able to evaluate the creditworthiness of firms.

    c.   are more subject to asymmetric information problems.

d. are more likely to emphasize short-run performance over long-run success.

e. would reduce competition in investment banking.

Topics for Discussion

1. Discuss the advantages and disadvantages of risk-related deposit-insurance premiums as a way to fix the deposit-insurance system.

2. How would higher capital-asset ratios and marking to market reduce the FDIC's liabilities in bank failures?

3. Who would win and who would lose if banks expanded into other businesses?

4. If foreign governments allow broader financial institutions, can U.S. banks remain competitive without the same broad powers?

5. How might requiring banks to hold secondary capital protect the FDIC?

6. What are the advantages and disadvantages of lowering the deposit ceiling?

7. Why did Congress put an end to the "too big to fail" policy?

8. What are the arguments for weakening the Glass-Steagall Act?

9. Why are bank holding companies excluded from holding commercial firms?

10. It is often argued that the twenty-first century will be knowledge-based and that the creation of new knowledge has significant economies of scale. What market structure is best suited to such a technology? What role would universal banks play in such an enviornment?

Exercise Questions

1. On June 16, 1992, the *Wall Street Journal* (p. B7) reported that a federal appeals court ruled that the 1933 National Banking Act prohibits Chase Manhattan, NA, from selling title insurance. A clause in the act forbids national banks to sell insurance unless they are located in a town with a population of less than 5,000. The Comptroller of the Currency had argued that selling title insurance was permitted since this activity was "incidental to banking."

a. Why do banks want to sell title insurance?

b. Who would oppose permitting banks to sell title insurance?

    c. What arguments might those opposed to letting banks sell title insurance put forth?

2. Jack Guttentag and Richard Herring have proposed a modification of the narrow banking plan. Rather than require banks to invest in government securities, banks could invest in any marketable assets, including corporate stocks. All assets would be marked to market.

    a. How does this proposal increase safety?

    b. Why would bank ownership of corporate stock likely be questioned?

Answer to Self-Tests

Completion

1.	Marking to market	8.	Narrow
2.	subordinated	9.	a firewall; Glass-Steagall Act
3.	a universal bank	10.	market
4.	"Too big to fail"	11.	lower
5.	higher	12.	Investment banks
6.	heterogeneous		
7.	insiders		

True-False

1.	True	7.	True
2.	False	8.	False
3.	True	9.	True
4.	True	10.	False
5.	False	11.	False
6.	False		

Multiple Choice

1.	*d*	7.	*c*
2.	*a*	8.	*c*
3.	*e*	9.	*c*
4.	*b*	10.	*f*
5.	*e*	11.	*c*
6.	*e*	12.	*a*

Answers to Exercise Questions

1a. Banks have been losing their traditional markets and are looking to enter new lines of business to increase profits. Banks may have a cost advantage over other firms in selling title insurance.

b. Land title insurance companies would oppose letting banks sell title insurance because they would not welcome competition for their turf.

c. Opponents would say that banks have an unfair edge because their source of funds (deposits) is subsidized by the government and that a conflict of interest would exist if banks were permitted to sell title insurance.

2a. Since the assets can be easily and quickly marked to market, regulators would have an excellent early warning system and might be able to close institutions before their net worth became negative.

b. Corporate stock is traditionally considered risky. Given the advent of highly variable interest rates, the relative risk may not be high. Another traditional argument is that banks with an equity position in a corporation may be more likely to grant loans. Since narrow banks make no corporate loans, this objection is removed.

CHAPTER 11   Central Banking

Learning Objectives

1. List the five chore and the three nonchore functions of the Fed.

2. Understand the historical context of the creation of the Fed in 1913.

3. Describe the formal and informal structure of the 12 Federal Reserve District Banks, the Board of Governors, and the Federal Open-Market Committee.

4. List the five sources of the Fed chariman's power.

5. Evaluate critically the independence of the Fed.

6. List the Fed's four constituencies.

7. Cite the five theories that explain central bank behavior.

Key Terms, Concepts, and Institutions

lender of last resort
central bank
Federal Reserve Bank
Board of Governors
Federal Open-Market Committee
discount rate
chore functions
public-choice theory

chairman of the Board
  of Governors
constituency
independence
open-market operations
political business cycle
partisan theory

Self-Test: Completion

1. The two most important functions of the Fed are _____ and

_____ .

2. Formally, the six class A and class B directors are elected by the _____ . Informally, they are often selected by the _____ .

3. The discount rate is set by the _____ , subject to approval by the Board of Governors.

4. Merger applications of member banks require the approval of _____ or _____ .

5. Checks are cleared by the _____ .

6. The most powerful single member of the FOMC is the _____ .

7. Monetary policy is decided mainly by the _____ .

8. Bank holding company acquisitions are approved by the _____ .

9. While the Fed does not lend to the government directly, it does so indirectly by using the _____ as an intermediary.

10. One important function of the 12 Federal Reserve Banks is to _____ and _____ the Fed's actions to the local business community.

11. Banks and the financial community, fixed-income groups, the financial press, and the academic economists are all major or minor components of the Fed's _____ .

12. Fed purchases and sales of securities are called _____ .

13. A central bank will buy its currency in the foreign-exchange market if the value of its currency is _____ the target range.

Self-Test: True-False

1. Congress sets the Fed's budget.

2. The Fed was originally envisioned as a loose confederation of 12 regionally dispersed banks each controlled by its own board of directors.

3. The federal-funds rate is the rate the Fed charges on its loans to banks and other depository institutions.

4. The stock of the Fed banks is owned by the member banks and pays a 6 percent return.

5. Most Federal Reserve Board members serve their full 14-year terms, so that there are only two vacancies on the Board every 4 years.

6. The text estimates that the chairman wields about 50 percent of the authority within the FOMC, while the other 50 percent is held by the other governors.

7. A major constituency of the Fed is composed of the fixed-income groups who stand to lose by inflation.

8. The President can send a cabinet member to attend the FOMC meetings.

9. The elections of class A and class B directors are vigorously contested.

10. We need a central bank because money will not manage itself.

11. The Fed fosters its independence from Congress and from political pressures in general by providing massive amounts of information.

Self-Test: Multiple Choice

1. When the Fed was created in 1913, its primary function was
   a. control of the money stock.
   b. lender of last resort.
   c. check clearing.
   d. bank examination.
   e. regulation of bank holding companies.

2. Which of the following is an argument for an independent Fed?
   a. Independence strengthens democracy.
   b. Independence allows policy coordination.
   c. Independence may allow the Fed to resist pressure from business and the unemployed to expand the money stock.
   d. The Fed has blundered in the past.
   e. The electorate can be educated to vote intelligently on monetary policy.

3. The Fed pays its bills
   a. through congressional appropriations.
   b. from its earnings on the stock market.
   c. from its ability to create reserves.
   d. from its earnings on securities.
   e. both c and d.

4. The Fed pursues all the following goals *except*
   a. a high rate of return for its stockholders.
   b. stable prices.
   c. high employment.
   d. bank safety.
   e. provision of finance to inner cities.

5. Federal Reserve Banks
   a. are commercial banks.
   b. independently set the discount rate for their own districts.
   c. make loans to institutions in their district.
   d. have presidents who dominate the FOMC.
   e. have presidents who usually have no influence in the selection of class A and class B directors.

6. The members of the Board of Governors usually serve
   a. all of their 14-year terms.
   b. at the pleasure of the President.
   c. until replaced by Congress.
   d. less than half their 14-year terms.
   e. until they retire.

7. All the following are chore functions of the Fed except
   a. acting as a banker's bank.
   b. clearing checks.
   c. controlling the money supply.
   d. issuing currency.
   e. examining banks.

8. All the following are sources of the Fed chairman's power *except* the chairman's
   a. ability to set the agenda for meetings.
   b. supervisory relationship with staff members of the board.
   c. ability to act as the board's representative to Congress and the President.
   d. leadership role at FOMC meetings.
   e. ability to interpose a veto in matters of FOMC policy.

9. The primary function of the Fed is now
   a. control of the money stock.
   b. to earn money for the Treasury.
   c. check clearing.
   d. bank examination.
   e. regulation of bank holding companies.

10. Which of the following Fed banks has a permanent seat on the FOMC?
   a. San Francisco
   b. Chicago
   c. St. Louis
   d. New York
   e. Richmond

Topics for Discussion

1. What are the goals of a central bank?

2. Describe the degree of congressional control over the Fed. Does Congress control the Fed's budget? Does the ownership of the Fed by its member banks weaken congressional control?

3. Is the Fed independent of the President? What channels of influence exist?

4. Should the Fed be independent? Should the chairman of the Board of Governors serve coterminously with the President? Should the FOMC be required to confer with Congress until a coordinated economic policy is formulated?

5. Should the Fed be required to explain and defend its policies? Would you support a requirement that all deliberations of the FOMC be a matter of public record?

6. Why is the Fed willing and able to act as a lender of last resort when other banks cannot or will not?

7. Why is the Fed's function as the lender of last resort less significant now than it was in 1913?

8. What functions does the Board of Governors serve independent of its FOMC membership?

9. What is the Fed's constituency? Is it so narrow that the Fed is unlikely to pursue the public interest?

10. Discuss the Fed chairman's sources of power.

Exercise Questions

1. Select the correct terms for this March 9, 1995, article in the *Wall Street Journal,* p. A16.

   . . . Central banks like strong currencies because they make prices of foreign goods and commodities, particularly energy, (cheaper/more expensive.) And that helps keep inflation (at a high level/at bay) at home. But business and fiscal planners worry that the export surge that drove the recovery in major European economies last year could ebb if European products become (cheaper/too expensive) abroad.

2.   . . . The Fed has been criticized for raising interest rates before seeing any evidence of worsening inflation, but Fed Chairman Alan Greenspan replied in remarks prepared for delivery over the weekend: 'If we had waited until inflation had become evident, it would have been too late. To successfully navigate a bend in the river, the barge must begin the turn well before the bend is reached,' Mr. Greenspan said, offering a new monetary-policy metaphor. 'Even so, currents are always changing and even an experienced crew cannot foresee all the events that might occur as the river is being navigated. A year ago, the Fed began its turn, and we do not yet know if it has been successful.' *Wall Street Journal,* January 30, 1995, p. A2.

What implications do Mr. Greenspan's remarks have for the political business cycle theory?

3.   . . . The battered dollar has new foes in Asia's central banks, whose coffers are overflowing with greenbacks earned by exporting goods to the U.S. . . . That's bad news for the dollar and the yen. . . . Japan now teeters on the edge of recession because of its strong currency, economists say . . . *Wall Street Journal,* April 12, 1995, p. C6.

   a.   To weaken the yen, the Bank of Japan should (raise/lower) its discount rate. The Bank of Japan might be reluctant to do this for fear of triggering (unemployment/inflation.)

   b.   To strengthen the dollar, the Fed would need to (raise/lower) U.S. interest rates. The Fed might be reluctant to do this for fear of triggering higher (unemployment/inflation.)

4.   If the Republicans succeed in controlling the White House and the Congress in the next election, what are the implications for monetary policy according to the partisan theory?

These two crossword puzzles are helpful reviews of the details of central banking introduced in this chapter.

Crossword Puzzle One

ACROSS

1.   Initially, the Fed was considered a _____ of banks to pool reserves.

2.   The Fed stands ready and _____ to act as a lender of last resort.

5. The Fed has gradually become more _____.
6. The number of people on the FOMC.
7. The number of people on the Boards of Directors.

8. _____ of Governors.
10. Garfield is one.
11. What the Fed ignores, but banks do not.
12. The European central bank to be established in 1993 is referred to as the

_____ .

DOWN

1. Another of the Fed's chore functions is to _____ .
3. What a central bank is not.
4. What member banks keep at Fed banks.
5. The most powerful member of the FOMC.

9. Examining banks is one of the Fed's _____ functions.

Crossword Puzzle Two

ACROSS

1. The group that determines monetary policy.
5. The rate of interest the Fed charges.
6. Where class B directors may be drawn from
8. Some wish Congress would _____ the Fed's purse strings.
9. A Fed chairman who does not have the "necessary ability" to avoid giving clear answers might be tempted to take the _____ amendment.
11. University of the Pacific.
12. What the Fed sells on the open market
13. and 14. The largest Fed bank is in _____ _____ .
              (13)   (14)

DOWN

2. The state with two Federal Reserve Banks.
3. Perhaps the Fed should not be independent, since it has made _____ in the past.
4. The Fed's support group.
5. If reserves _____ , the Fed must act as a lender of last resort.
7. It stole Christmas.
9. What the Fed does to fraud.
10. Used by gardeners and firefighters.

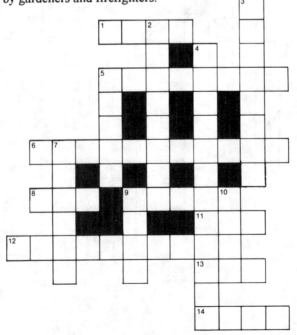

Answers to Self-Tests

Completion

1. controlling the money supply, preventing bank failures
2. member banks; President of the Fed bank
3. 12 Federal Reserve Banks
4. the Board of Governors of the Fed, a Reserve Bank
5. Fed Banks
6. chairman
7. FOMC
8. Board of Governors of the Fed
9. public
10. explain, justify
11. constituency
12. open-market operations
13. below

True-False

1.	False	7.	True
2.	True	8.	False
3.	False	9.	False
4.	True	10.	True
5.	False	11.	True
6.	False		

Multiple Choice

1.	b	6.	d
2.	c	7.	c
3.	e	8.	e
4.	a	9.	a
5.	c	10.	d

Answers to Exercise Questions

1. cheaper; at bay; too expensive
2. Mr. Greenspan's remarks imply that the Fed cannot play the political business cycle game because the lag in the effect of monetary policy is too hard to estimate.
3. a. lower; inflation
   b. raise; unemployment
4. The partisan theory suggests that the top priority for monetary policy should be controlling inflation.

Answer to Crossword Puzzle One

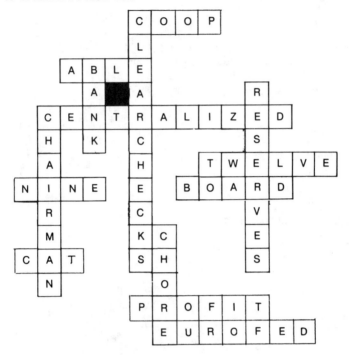

Answer to Crossword Puzzle Two

CHAPTER 12   The Measurement of Money

Learning Objectives

1. Understand the empirical and a priori approaches to defining money.

2. Come to terms with the problems of defining money in a rapidly changing financial environment.

3. Recognize that what we choose to call "money" may be unimportant but that describing the variable the Fed can control to affect nominal income is important.

4. Gain some appreciation for the practical difficulties of actually measuring money.

5. Identify the components of *M-1*, *M-2*, and *M-3*.

Key Terms, Concepts, and Institutions

a priori	*M-1A*
empirical	negotiable
M-1	near-money
M-2	narrow money
M-3	broad money
monetary services index	seasonal adjustment
weighted average	underground economy

Self-Test: Completion

1. The a priori approach to defining money focuses on money as the

   _____ .

2. *M-1A* consists of currency and those checkable deposits that

   _____ .

3. The approach that focuses on the relationship between money and nominal income is called the _____ approach to the definition of money.

4. If we construct a monetary aggregate that assigns greater weight to assets with lower interest rates, the aggregate is called a _____ .

5. Credit is not money because credit is not _____ .

6. While *M-1* includes most currency, cash in _____ is excluded.

7. All definitions of money exclude deposits held by _____ .

8. Large time deposits are _____ ; this means that they can be sold in the secondary market.

9. People in the _____ make payments in currency so that their illegal activities will be harder to trace.

10. Since different financial instruments have different degrees of moneyness, perhaps we ought to construct a definition of money that is a

    _____ .

Self-Test: True-False

1. The dispute between the supporters of an a priori definition of money and an empirical definition is a dispute about how the economy operates.

2. An example of a near-money is a credit card line of credit.

3. The weighted aggregate discussed in the text gives a greater weight to assets that pay higher interest rates.

4. Cash items in the process of collection are deducted from the definition of money on the assumption that those who wrote the checks have already deducted the amount from their records.

5. Interbank deposits are included in the definition of money.

6. The a priori definition of money focuses on those attributes of money that make the money supply important for macroeconomic policy.

7. The demand for money always declines at Christmas.

8. At present, the Fed primarily uses *M-1* to formulate policy.

9. The empirical definition of money tries to identify the concept of money that has the greatest influence on income, whether or not money thus conceived can be controlled by the Fed.

10. *M-1A* measures better than *M-1* those funds that are held just as a medium of exchange.

Self-Test: Multiple Choice

1. Currency is included in
    a. *M-1.*
    b. *M-2.*
    c. *M-3.*
    d. all the above.
    e. none of the above.

2. Money-market deposit accounts are included in
    a. *M-1, M-2,* and *M-3.*
    b. only *M-1.*
    c. only *M-3.*
    d. *M-2* and *M-3.*
    e. only *M-2.*

3. Narrow money
    a. consists of items that can be spent immediately.
    b. includes small time deposits.
    c. is also called *M-2.*
    d. is presently used by the Fed to formulate policy.
    e. includes those money-market deposit accounts against which a limited number of checks can be written.

4. Savings deposits are included in *M-2* but not *M-1* because savings deposits
    a. earn a higher rate of interest than the deposits in *M-1.*
    b. are held in thrift institutions.
    c. are not media of exchange.
    d. have a penalty for early withdrawal.
    e. are not wealth.

5. Large time deposits
   a. are nonnegotiable.
   b. are included in *M-2*.
   c. can be redeemed at face value.
   d. are time deposits greater than $100,000.
   e. are a component of narrow money.

6. All the following are excluded from the money stock *except*
   a. state and local government deposits.
   b. interbank deposits.
   c. vault cash.
   d. U.S. government deposits.
   e. cash items in the process of collection.

7. Which of the following is excluded from *M-2*?
   a. traveler's checks
   b. term Eurodollars
   c. overnight repurchase agreements
   d. checkable deposits
   e. money-market deposit accounts

8. Which of the following cannot be considered near-money?
   a. credit cards
   b. overdraft privileges
   c. foreign currencies
   d. traveler's checks
   e. Treasury bills

9. Given that there are different degrees of moneyness it makes sense to
   a. use the inverse of the yield of different forms of money to construct a weighted aggregate.
   b. define money as the inverse of the price level.
   c. measure different kinds of money by how much gold they can buy.
   d. give a higher weight to money with a longer time period to maturity.
   e. give a higher weight to money with more restrictions on its use.

10. The a priori definition of money focuses on
    a. money as the unit of account.
    b. money as the store of value.
    c. the impact of money on nominal income.
    d. money as the medium of exchange.
    e. all the above.

11. The difference in the amount of currency issued by the Treasury and the amount held by households can be explained by
    a. the underground economy.
    b. lost currency.
    c. currency that has been destroyed.
    d. currency held in foreign countries.
    e. all the above.

Topics for Discussion

1. Why is it important to define money?

2. How would you change the definition of money if it became permissible to write an unlimited number of checks directly against money-market funds?

3. How would you change the definition of money if the government issued a limited number of ration stamps for various commodities? (To buy the good, you would need both the stamp and the full cash price.)

4. Argue for a weighted average as the definition of money.

5. Argue against a weighted average as the definition of money.

6. Should the Fed stop seasonally adjusting the monetary aggregates, since the seasonal adjustments are subject to such large errors?

7. Discuss the advantages and disadvantages of using $M-1$ and $M-2$ as measures of money.

8. Why not define money as "reserves of banks and other depository institutions," since the Fed has control of these aggregates?

Exercise Questions

1. Table 12.1 lists the components of the different monetary aggregates in billions of dollars for February 1995. Your task is to construct the aggregates themselves.

Table 12.1 Components of Monetary Aggregates, Febrary 1995

Components of monetary aggregates	Billions of dollars
Currency	$357.0
Traveler's checks	8.1
Demand deposits	375.0
Other checkable deposits	394.0
Small time deposits	852.2
Savings deposits and money-market deposit accounts	1,105.0
Money-market mutual funds (general purpose and broker-dealer)	397.0
Overnight repurchase agreements and overnight Eurodollars	119.3
Large time deposits	371.1
Term repurchase agreements and term Eurodollars	170.3
Money-market mutual funds (institution only)	118.1

Source: *Federal Reserve Bulletin*, May 1995, p. A14.

Adding the appropriate components, we find that

a. *M-1* is $ _____ billion.

b. *M-2* is $ _____ billion.

c. *M-3* is $ _____ billion.

2. Put an X next to items that are included *only* in *M-3:*

_____ time deposits over $100,000
_____ currency
_____ overnight Eurodollars
_____ term repurchase agreements
_____ other checkable deposits
_____ term Eurodollars
_____ savings deposits
_____ money-market mutual funds (institutions only)
_____ small time deposits
_____ money-market deposit accounts

3. List the items below under the appropriate measure of money. Some items will be used more than once.

other checkable deposits money-market mutual-fund balances
money-market mutual funds overnight Eurodollars
demand deposits savings deposits
currency traveler's checks
large time deposits money-market deposit accounts
term Eurodollars overnight repurchase agreements
small time deposits term repurchase agreements

a. M-1:

b. M-2:

b. M-3:

Answers to Self-Tests

Completion

1. medium of exchange
2. do not pay interest
3. empirical
4. monetary services index
5. wealth
6. bank vaults
7. the U.S. government
8. negotiable
9. underground economy
10. weighted aggregate

True-False

1. False
2. True
3. False
4. True
5. False
6. False
7. False
8. False
9. False
10. True

Multiple Choice

1. *d*	7. *b*
2. *d*	8. *d*
3. *a*	9. *a*
4. *c*	10. *d*
5. *d*	11. *e*
6. *a*	

Answers to Exercise Questions

1. *a.* 1134.1
   b. 3607.6
   c. 4337.8

2. __X__ time deposits over $100,000
   _____ currency
   _____ overnight Eurodollars
   __X__ term repurchase agreements
   _____ other checkable deposits
   __X__ term Eurodollars
   _____ savings deposits
   __X__ money-market mutual funds (institutions only)
   _____ small time deposits
   _____ money-market deposit accounts

3a. M-1: Currency, demand deposits, other checkable deposits, traveler's checks

b. M-2: Currency, demand deposits, other checkable deposits, traveler's checks, small time deposits, money-market deposit accounts, savings deposits, money-market mutual-fund balances, overnight repurchase agreements, overnight Eurodollars

c. M-3: Currency, demand deposits, other checkable deposits, traveler's checks, small time deposits, money-market deposit accounts, savings deposits, money-market mutual-fund balances (general purpose & broker/dealers), overnight repurchase agreements, overnight Eurodollars, large time deposits, term Eurodollars, term repurchase agreements, money-market mutual funds

CHAPTER 13   The Creation of Money

Learning Objectives

1. Explain the process of multiple deposit creation and contraction.

2. Explain the connection between loan creation and deposit creation.

3. Understand how leakages such as excess reserves, deposits into currency, and checkable deposits into time deposits affect the money multiplier and the deposit creation process.

4. Use the money multiplier formulas to find M-1 and M-2.

5. State which factors affect the leakage coefficients e, k, and t.

6. Explain why, in the absence of Fed action, the money supply would behave procyclically.

7. Explain the "New View" of money creation.

Key Terms, Concepts, and Institutions

reserves (R)
required reserves
excess reserves
T accounts
currency drain
multiple deposit creation
deposit multiplier
reserve–demand deposit ratio
excess reserve–demand deposit
   ratio (e)
currency–demand deposit
   ratio (k)

required reserve–demand deposit
   ratio (rr)
money multiplier
multiple deposit contraction
time deposit—demand deposit
   ratio (t)
excess reserve ratio against
   time deposits (e_t)
endogenous money view
deposits
leakages
money-supply theory

Extra Help: A Closer Look at the Money Multipliers

Why are there so many varieties of money multipliers and how do you keep them straight? To begin, you should realize that all money multipliers relate some variable that the Fed controls more or less directly with some definition of money. There are as many multipliers as there are combinations of variables controlled by the Fed and definitions of money. Realizing that all the money multipliers have the same basic structure can help you keep them straight. Once you learn this, you'll see that all the varieties are straightforward adaptations. You may even find it fun to invent your own money multiplier.

The equation below applies to all money multipliers. Let B represent the variable directly controlled by the Fed and M the chosen definition of money.

$$M = \frac{M/D}{B/D} B. \tag{1}$$

Since the D's cancel out of the numerator and denominator, D could refer to anything. D is always some definition of deposits, but it could be daiquiris or daffodils and still be mathematically correct. The numerator M/D is often broken down into component parts. For example, if money is defined as deposits plus currency, then the numerator would be written as $(D + C)/D = D/D + C/D = 1 + C/D$. This, and most other texts, let k represent the currency to deposit ratio, so the numerator is $1 + k$. Our generic multiplier could refer to any definition of money because deposits may be broadly defined to include savings deposits, small denomination time deposits, and so on, or narrowly defined to exclude them. If the definition of deposits in M is broader than the definition of D, then additional terms will appear in the numerator.

The denominator B/D can also be broken down into its component parts. For example, if B refers to required reserves, excess reserves, and currency, then the denominator becomes $rr + e + k$, the ratios of required reserves, excess reserves, and currency to deposits. In the text, excess reserves are broken down even further, into excess reserves held against demand deposits and excess reserves held against time deposits, so that the denominator becomes $rr + e + k + te_t$.

Let's see if you understand the basic format now: It is traditional to start with a very simple definition of B. Let's assume that only required reserves exist so that the denominator is simply rr. As more elements are added to B, the denominator gets more complicated. Similarly, it is common to begin with deposit multipliers and build up to money multipliers so that the numerator is initially just 1, the deposit-deposit ratio, and becomes more complex as more types of deposits or currency are added to the definition of M.

While this should help keep the formulas straight, don't let the details obscure the main points. The arithmetic is used to illustrate and explain how the behavior of banks and depositors influences the overall money supply. People decide how much currency to hold relative to deposits, and this influences k. Bankers decide how many excess reserves to hold, and this influences e. The more complicated forms of the multiplier allow the effects of depositor and banker behavior to be brought into the analysis. The reason we define D as deposits and not daffodils or daiquiris is that we are interested in the sober and unromantic decisions of bankers and depositors.

Self-Test: Completion

1. As long as a depository institution has _____ , it can create more loans and deposits, should it choose to do so.

2. Multiple deposit creation does not occur if 100 percent reserves are required or if loans are made in _____ only.

3. If the required reserve ratio is 10 percent and the Fed writes a check for $20,000, the bank that presents the check to the Fed can now make an additional \$_____ worth of loans, should it choose to do so.

4. Frightened Fred withdraws $10,000 from his savings and loan association. If the savings and loan holds no excess reserves and the required reserve ratio is 30 percent, then the savings and loan must acquire \$_____ in additional reserves.

5. Fred's savings and loan association can get the needed reserves by selling _____ the bank holds, calling in a _____ , or borrowing reserves from the Fed.

6. While depository institutions with inadequate reserves would prefer to meet reserve requirements by obtaining more _____ , for all depository institutions jointly, this option is controlled by the Fed. Instead, depository institutions may be forced to reduce _____ .

7. If tax rates were to increase or if illegal transactions such as drug trafficking and prostitution were to increase, then the currency-deposit ratio k would _____ and the money stock and deposit level would _____ assuming $R + C$ is held constant.

8. If the Fed increases reserves, the marginal cost of servicing deposits _____ .

9. Loans are recorded on the _____ -hand side of the bank's T account.

10. Loans are an _____ of the bank because they represent a claim on someone's future assets.

11. The Fed may try to expand the money supply when interest rates rise. If so, we say money is _____ .

Self-Test: True-False

1. The Fed can control reserves.

2. Since the public decides how much currency to hold, the Fed cannot control $R + C$.

3. An increase in the excess reserve ratio e reduces M-1.

4. To construct M-1, we multiply demand deposits by $1 + k + t$.

5. Money supply theory allows e, k, and t to vary.

6. An increase in the interest rate tends to reduce e.

7. We can associate $R + C$ with the multiplier $1/rr$, even if currency and excess reserves exist.

8. If demand deposits equal $1 billion and $t = 2$, then time deposits equal $2 billion.

9. If $rr + e = k$ and $R + C$ is $1 billion, then currency equals $.5 billion.

10. In our system, as the money supply increases, bank loans decrease.

11. Recessions are defined more by rising unemployment than by high unemployment.

Self-Test: Multiple Choice

The next several questions lead you through the implications of an increase in the money supply. Forget formulas for a moment, here we emphasize ideas.

1. If the Fed wants to increase the money supply, it generally begins by
   a. buying shares of publicly traded corporations.
   b. buying bonds issued by private companies.
   c. buying bonds originally issued by the government and currently owned by a private bond dealer.
   d. selling yen.
   e. asking the Treasury to increase deficit spending.

2. The Fed check used to make the purchase above is deposited in a bank, which presents the check to the Fed in exchange for
   a. vault cash or reserves at the Fed.
   b. Treasury bills.
   c. stock certificates.
   d. commercial paper.
   e. yen

3. The bank above finds it has the wherewithal to make additional loans, so it
   a. raises interest rates to attract loan customers.
   b. loans funds to people who would have been considered too risky before.
   c. increases requirements for making loans.
   d. lowers interest rates.
   e. both b and d.
   f. both a and c.

4. As loans are taken out, spending increases. This leads to
   a. higher prices and less production.
   b. higher prices and more production.
   c. lower prices.
   d. unemployment.
   e. a trade surplus.

5. The Fed worries about balancing the positive and negative effects of monetary expansion. Which of the following is unambiguously a negative effect of monetary expansion?
   a. lower prices
   b. higher production
   c. a trade surplus and a rising dollar value
   d. higher prices
   e. increased risk-taking by banks

But the Fed isn't the only player in the money market, so it must consider its moves in the context of moves by other players. This is where the money multiplier comes in. Now remember that $D + C = [(1 + k)/(rr + e + k + te_t)](R + C)$.

6. If banks take more risk and hold fewer excess reserves, then
   a. C rises and money supply rises.
   b. e declines and the smaller denominator implies $D + C$ increases.
   c. k declines as $D + C$ does.
   d. t declines as $D + C$ does.
   e. rr declines as $D + C$ does.

7. If business loan demand increased, then depository institutions would probably borrow _____ reserves from the Fed. Unless the Fed offset this, the money supply would _____ .
   a. more; increase
   b. more; decrease
   c. less; increase
   d. less; decrease
   e. less; not change

8. At Christmastime the public tends to have a _____ currency-deposit ratio. This, if $R + C$ is constant, would _____ the money supply.
   a. higher; increase
   b. higher; decrease
   c. lower; increase
   d. lower; decrease
   e. lower; not change

9. If banks raise their interest on time deposits but leave the demand deposit rate unchanged, then
   a. C rises and money supply rises.
   b. e declines and $D + C$ increases.
   c. k declines as $D + C$ does.
   d. t rises and $D + C$ declines.
   e. rr rises and $D + C$ declines.

10. According to the endogenous money view,
   a. the Fed should control $R + C$ and not reserves.
   b. the multiplier approach is too mechanical and leaves out too much that is known about the behavior of depository institutions and the public.
   c. the multiplier approach worked before the 1980 Monetary Control Act but needs a major overhaul now.
   d. the interest rate effects on t and k can be ignored.
   e. banks and the public—not the Fed—control the money supply.

Topics for Discussion

1. In what ways do banks profit from the money creation process?

2. After the Great Depression and the bank runs associated with it, banks maintained unusually large levels of excess reserves. What might explain this?

3. In the mid-1930s the Fed believed the large levels of excess reserves meant the Fed no longer controlled the money supply. They believed any variation in reserve availability would simply be absorbed in a changing excess reserve level. Do you agree?

4. Use the multipliers to explain the seasonal variation in deposits due to an increased currency demand at Christmas. Does this give you an idea about how the seasonal fluctuation could be identified and removed from the data?

5. How might changes in capital requirements affect the multiplier process?

6. How would massive loan losses affect the money creation process?

7. If it were necessary for the Fed to act as a lender of last resort on a massive scale, could it combat inflation at the same time?

Exercise Questions

1. Suppose there is only one kind of depository account with a reserve requirement of 10 percent, no use of currency, and, ultimately, full loaning of excess reserves by banks.

    In this economy, the Fed writes a $100,000 check to a securities dealer named Alice. She deposits the check in her account at Bank A. Record the changes in her bank's T account at this stage.

Bank A

Assets	Liabilities
reserves (a: $_____)	deposits (b: $_____)

Now excess reserves are (c: $_____) and the excess reserve–deposit level is (d: $_____). Our formula correctly implies the change in reserves equals the change in deposits since $rr + e = $ (e: _____) + (f: _____), so that the multiplier is (g: _____).

Bank A loans out the excess (h: $_____) to Allen, an artichoke grower. Allen uses the money to hire Bambi, an independent trucker, to haul the produce to market. Bambi banks at Bank B. Bank B credits Bambi's account and clears the check through the Fed. The Fed transfers reserves from Bank A to Bank B. After the reserve transfer, the T accounts for the two banks look like;

Bank A

Assets	Liabilities
reserves (*i*: $_____) loans (*k*: $_____)	deposits (*j*: $_____)

Bank B

Assets	Liabilities
reserves (*l*: $_____)	deposits (*m*: $_____)

Bank B has excess reserves of (*n*: $_____). If this is loaned out, Bank C will find it has (*o*: $_____) it could loan out. The process ends when (*p*: $_____) of new deposits have been created. This can be found by plugging in (*q*: _____) for *e* in our formula. It is also the sum of a geometric progression.

2. Let's adapt the example to allow for currency and excess reserves. Assume $rr + t(rr_t) = .1$, $e = .05$, and $k = .1$. The Fed check of $100,000 increases $R + C$ by (*a*: $_____). If we multiply this by 1 over

(*b*: _____ + _____ + _____), we have the change in deposits once the banks and the public are again holding the currency and excess reserves they desire. Thus deposits change by

(*c*: $_____). Since currency and required reserves both equal 10 percent of deposits, currency must have increased by

(*d*: $_____) and required reserves must have increased by

(*e*: $_____) while excess reserves at 5 percent of deposits must have increased by (*f*: $_____). Notice that their sum is equal to the change in $R + C$.

Now that we know that the total reserves have increased by

(*g*: $_____), we can use the multiplier for reserves, which is 1

over (*h*: _____ + _____). Therefore the reserve

multiplier is (*i*: _____). Multiplying the reserves by the reserve multiplier, we find the change in deposits, which is (*j:* $_____). Even more simply, we could have multiplied the change in required reserves of (*k:* $_____) times 1/*rr* and found that deposits changed by (*l:* $_____). So we see that if we know the change in reserves, required reserves, or $R + C$, their associated multipliers will all give the change in deposits. However, it is often easier to find the change in $R + C$ than the change in any single component.

Answers to Self-Tests

Completion

1.	excess reserves	7.	increase, decrease
2.	cash	8.	declines
3.	$18,000	9.	left
4.	$7,000	10.	asset
5.	securities; loan	11.	endogenous
6.	reserves; deposits		

True-False

1.	True	7.	False
2.	False	8.	True
3.	True	9.	True
4.	False	10.	False
5.	True	11.	True
6.	True		

Multiple Choice

1.	c	6.	b
2.	a	7.	a
3.	e	8.	b
4.	b	9.	d
5.	d	10.	b

Answers to Exercise Questions

1.	a.	100,000	e.	.1
	b.	100,000	f.	.9
	c.	90,000	g.	1
	d.	.9	h.	90,000

	i.	10,000		n.	81,000
	j.	100,000		o.	72,900
	j̸.	90,000		p.	1,000,000
	l.	90,000		q.	0
	m.	90,000			
2.	a.	100,000		g.	60,000
	b.	.1, .05, .1		h.	.1, .05
	c.	400,000		i.	6.67
	d.	40,000		j.	400,000
	e.	40,000		k.	40,000
	f.	20,000		l.	400,000

CHAPTER 14   Bank Reserves and Related Measures

Learning Objectives

1. Understand the mechanism by which the Fed controls the base, reserves, and the money supply.

2. Recognize that while actions by the Treasury, the public, banks, and foreign central banks all affect the various reserve measures, the Fed is able to offset these effects.

3. Understand why the Fed's control over the base is not perfect in the short run.

Key Terms, Concepts, and Institutions

borrowings from the Fed
float
base
free reserves
unborrowed (owned) reserves
excess reserves

adjusted (extended) base and capital
market factors
total reserves
unborrowed base
other Fed liabilities

Self-Test: Completion

1. Bad weather can increase reserves by increasing _____ .

2. If the Fed intervenes in foreign-exchange markets to buy Swiss francs, then the Fed check _____ both reserves and the base.

3. Total reserves less reserves held at the Fed equals _____ .

4. As the Fed clears a check, sometimes the reserves of the bank presenting the check are increased before the reserves of the bank it is drawn on are reduced. This is called _____ .

5. The monetary base consists of _____ and _____ .

6. As average reserve requirements fall, the adjusted base _____ .

7. Excess reserves equal total reserves minus _____ .

8. Excess reserves minus borrowed reserves equal _____ .

9. Those factors that can change reserves but are beyond the Fed's control are called _____ .

10. The unborrowed base equals the monetary base minus _____ .

Self-Test: True-False

1. An increase in free reserves means deposits have increased.

2. The money stock increases when the Fed buys paper clips.

3. An increase in Treasury currency held by the public ultimately decreases reserves.

4. If a new member bank buys Fed stock, reserves fall.

5. When the Treasury shifts tax funds that have been collecting in depository institutions to its Fed account, reserves increase.

6. Unless the money multiplier is a constant, the Fed cannot control the money supply by controlling reserves.

7. The money multipliers for the adjusted base have been rising steadily.

8. Monetary policy can still be expansionary even if the base has not changed.

9. If depository institutions rapidly repay any borrowed reserves rather than use them to finance additional loans, then deposit creation depends more on unborrowed reserves than on total reserves.

Self-Test: Multiple Choice

Table 14.1 Selected Fed Data: Daily Averages in Millions for the Two Weeks Ending May 24, 1995

Total reserves	$ 57,746
Required reserves	56,929
Borrowings from the Fed	144
Monetary base	431,578

Source: *The Wall Street Journal*, May 26, 1995, p. C14.

1. According to Table 14.1, excess reserves were
   a. $431,434 million.
   b. $673 million.
   c. $817 million.
   d. $57,692 million.
   e. $373,382 million.

2. According to Table 14.1, unborrowed reserves were
   a. $431,434 million.
   b. $673 million.
   c. $817 million.
   d. $57,692 million.
   e. $373,382 million.

3. According to Table 14.1, currency in circulation was
   a. $431,434 million.
   b. $673 million.
   c. $817 million.
   d. $57,692 million.
   e. $373,382 million.

4. According to Table 14.1, the unborrowed base was
   a. $431,434 million.
   b. $673 million.
   c. $817 million.
   d. $57,692 million.
   e. $373,382 million.

5. According to Table 14.1, free reserves were
   a. $431,434 million.
   b. $673 million.
   c. $817 million.

    d. $57,692 million.

    e. $373,382 million.

6. All of the following increase reserves *except*
   a. a decrease in other Fed liabilities and capital.
   b. a decrease in Treasury currency held by the public.
   c. an increase in other Fed assets.
   d. an increase in the gold stock.
   e. none of the above; all increase reserves.

7. An increase in other Federal reserve liabilities
   a. increases reserves because the Fed has to buy the liabilities.
   b. increases reserves because Fed liabilities are currency and currency is reserves.
   c. decreases reserves because it represents assets acquired but not paid for.
   d. decreases reserves because it is a technical adjustment to avoid double counting Treasury currency.
   e. does not change reserves.

8. When the Fed writes a check which of the following increases?
   a. reserves
   b. unborrowed reserves
   c. the base
   d. the unborrowed base
   e. all the above.

9. An increase in currency in circulation _____ reserves and

   _____ the base.
   a. increases, increases
   b. increases, decreases
   c. decreases, increases
   d. decreases, decreases
   e. decreases, does not change

10. Free reserves are
    a. interest-free loans from the Fed to unprofitable institutions.
    b. reserves that the institution is free to use to make loans.
    c. excess reserves less borrowed reserves.
    d. always positive.
    e. always positive when deposits are increasing.

Topics for Discussion

1. On June 14, 1983, the *Wall Street Journal* reported that news of open-market sales of securities had sent jitters through the financial community on June 13 until news of large Fed loans to troubled Seattle First National Bank were announced. Analysts then concluded the reserve draining operation was a technical adjustment and not a sign of a policy change. Explain.

2. How is it possible for free reserves to fall and reserves to rise?

3. Why does the Fed prefer to watch unborrowed reserves and the unborrowed base?

Exercise Questions

1. Use the changes in various Fed accounts listed in Table 14.2 to calculate the change in reserves from May 17 to May 24, 1995 (millions of dollars).

Table 14.2 Member Bank Reserve Changes, May 17 to May 24, 1995 (millions of dollars)

Purchases of U.S. government and federal agency issues	$ 911 +915
Borrowings from the Fed	10
Float	−128
Other Fed assets	−1,116
Gold stock	
SDR certificates	
Treasury currency outstanding	14
Currency in circulation	−500
Treasury cash holdings	−11 +11
Treasury, foreign, and other deposits with Federal Reserve banks	−751
Service related balances, adjusted	1
Other Fed liabilities	−45

Source: *Wall Street Journal*, May 26, 1995, p. C14.

2. Fill in the table below, using a + if the event results in an increase in reserves and a – to indicate that the event results in a decrease in reserves.

Event	Result
a. The float decreases	
b. Treasury cash holdings decrease	
c. Foreign governments transfer funds at depository institutions to their accounts at the Fed	
d. Other Federal Reserve assets increase	

Answers to Self-Tests

Completion

1. float
2. increases
3. vault cash
4. float
5. reserves of depository institutions, currency held by the public
6. rises
7. required reserves
8. free reserves
9. market factors
10. borrowings from the Fed

True-False

1. False
2. True
3. True
4. True
5. False
6. False
7. False
8. True
9. True

Multiple Choice

1. c
2. d
3. e
4. a
5. b
6. e
7. c
8. e
9. e
10. c

Answers to Exercise Questions

1. Draw a line between Treasury currency outstanding and currency in circulation. Add up the numbers above the line and subtract the numbers below the line. Reserves increased by $997 million.

2.

	Event	Result
a.	The float decreases	−
b.	Treasury cash holdings decrease	+
c.	Foreign governments transfer funds at depository institutions to their accounts at the Fed	−
d.	Other Federal Reserve assets increase	+

CHAPTER 15   The Determinants of
                Aggregate Expenditures

Learning Objectives

1. Use either the Keynesian or monetarist approach to explain variations in aggregate expenditures.

2. Explain how the Cambridge and quantity theory approaches lead to different variables as the causes of fluctuations in aggregate expenditures.

3. Use a 45-degree diagram to illustrate the impact of changes in investment, consumption, and government taxing and spending policies on aggregate expenditures and production.

4. Explain how the interaction of the multiplier and accelerator could lead to economic instability.

5. Explain the user cost of capital.

Key Terms, Concepts, and Institutions

Keynesians	transactions velocity
monetarists	autonomous consumption
consumption	marginal propensity to consume
investment	disposable income
government spending	permanent income
net exports	user cost
velocity (or income velocity)	depreciation
real vs. nominal income	capital coefficient

126

quantity theory of money
Cambridge equation
q theory

accelerator
investment multiplier
risk premium

Self-Test: Completion

1. Keynesians link aggregate expenditures to _____ , while monetarists link aggregate expenditures to _____ .

2. In the Keynesian approach, output retained by business is called _____ . (Notice that this excludes bonds and stocks, included in the common usage of the term.)

3. Income after personal taxes have been deducted is called

    _____ .

4. The _____ theory argues that consumption depends on anticipated income as well as current income.

5. The user cost of capital has four components. They are

    _____ , which reflects the change in the value of capital over time; _____ , which reflects the cost of borrowed funds;

    _____ , which compensates for uncertainty; and

    _____ , which is wholly dependent on government decisions.

6. Investment less depreciation is _____ .

7. Firms can raise money by selling their accounts receivable; this is called

    _____ .

8. Exports less imports are _____ .

9. Higher prices increase _____ income but not _____ income.

10. The interaction of the multiplier and the _____ could cause income to shoot up or down dramatically.

11. If government spending rises by $1 billion, the marginal propensity to consume c is .75, and investment is unchanged, then income should

    rise by $_____ billion.

12. According to the quantity theory, the Federal Reserve determines the
    _____ money supply, while the public determines the
    _____ money supply.

13. After an increase in the supply of money, the demand for money rises
    first due to a decline in _____ and later due to increases in
    either _____ or _____ . If income is fixed at full
    employment, then, ultimately, any increase in the supply of money is
    absorbed through increases in _____ .

Self-Test: True-False

1. Most economists attribute fluctuations in nominal and real GDPs
   primarily to fluctuations in the capacity to produce.

2. Income velocity measures the number of times a dollar is spent, on
   average, within a given period.

3. Transactions velocity includes spending on intermediate products and is
   therefore greater than income velocity.

4. $Y = C + I + G + X$ because all production Y must eventually end up in
   the hands of households C, businesses I, government G, or foreigners X.

5. If actual investment is greater than desired investment, then there is an
   unintended depletion of inventories.

6. It may be important to include both current and permanent income in
   the consumption function if households cannot borrow enough against
   their future income.

7. Capital is a flow, whereas investment is a stock.

8. A firm's net investment must be positive just to maintain its current
   output.

9. The economy should be more stable if consumption depends on
   permanent income rather than on current income.

10. The investment multiplier applies only to investment and not to changes
    in government spending.

11. Higher taxes reduce the multiplier because each dollar earned has a
    smaller impact on disposable income and the next round of spending.

12. According to the q theory, if stock prices rise, then the market value of corporations increases and firms are more likely to buy existing companies than to build new ones.

13. The 1987 stock market crash caused large changes in consumption.

Self-Test: Multiple Choice

1. The Cambridge equation and the quantity equation are different because the Cambridge
   a. k and income velocity often move independently of each other.
   b. k emphasizes the mechanics of transactions rather than human decision making.
   c. k leads us to consider income and the opportunity cost of holding money as important determinants of aggregate expenditures.
   d. k leads us to consider technology and the speed with which transactions can be conducted as important determinants of aggregate expenditures.
   e. approach denies the importance of money as a factor affecting aggregate expenditures.

2. Compared to income velocity, transactions velocity
   a. is more commonly used because we have better data on transactions than on income.
   b. is lower because much income is generated without transactions.
   c. is only a tautology. No assumptions need to be added to income velocity to make it a useful theory.
   d. focuses on the less-interesting variable (transactions).
   e. is less heavily affected by stock market sales and used car sales.

3. We expect savings to fall and consumption to rise if
   a. the middle-aged become a larger share of the population.
   b. wealth increases.
   c. a religious movement that denounces material possessions expands.
   d. social security programs are repealed.
   e. people become convinced their incomes will fall.

4. Higher real interest rates affect consumption by
   a. rewarding savings more heavily.
   b. increasing the value of securities that households hold.
   c. increasing a household's liquidity.
   d. reducing the opportunity cost of purchasing consumer durables.
   e. relaxing credit rationing.

5. The user cost of capital increases if
   a. over time the firm's ratio of debt to net worth falls.
   b. the breakdown of international trade agreements increases uncertainty.
   c. bond prices rise.
   d. stock prices rise.
   e. the government increases tax breaks for investment.

6. The acceleration principle results from the fact that
   a. investment by one firm leads to increased demand for other firms' products and more investment by other firms.
   b. the capital stock is generally several times output, so that an increase in desired output leads to a multiplied increase in desired capital.
   c. business expansion increases employment and consumption.
   d. once stock prices begin to fall, they are expected to fall, so investors sell them.
   e. success by one firm increases optimism.

7. Accelerator effects may not be particularly strong because
   a. rapidly expanding the capital stock is more expensive than a slow expansion.
   b. expansions by several firms simultaneously can significantly increase the cost of capital goods.
   c. even if current output rises significantly, anticipated output may not change much.
   d. the investment process can disrupt the firm's other activities, especially if the firm embarks on a crash program.
   e. all the above.

8. The economy will tend to be more stable if
   a. the capital coefficient is large.
   b. the multiplier is large.
   c. income increases are assumed to be permanent.
   d. our ability to predict the future yield of investment improves.
   e. consumption depends only on current income.

9. According to the quantity theory equation,
   a. if the money stock rises and velocity is constant, then income rises but not prices.
   b. if money and velocity are constant, an increase in income implies a reduction in prices.
   c. if the stock of money rises and velocity declines, we do not know how prices and income vary.

    d.   if velocity and income are constant, then doubling the money supply must double prices.

    e.   all but *a.*

10. Investment increases if
    a.   the risk premium increases.
    b.   anticipated sales increase.
    c.   debt–net worth ratios increase.
    d.   interest rates increase.
    e.   all the above.

11. According to the text, if the supply of money is increased, "firms and households now find they hold more money than they want to."
    a.   This must be a joke. No one ever has too much money.
    b.   Whenever anyone buys something, he gives away money. In this sense, money can be excess: a person can prefer the goods and services to the money.
    c.   As the money is spent, the interest rate on bonds tends to rise due to increased demand.
    d.   As the excess is spent, income increases, and so money demand decreases.
    e.   As the excess is spent, prices fall.

12. Of the various components of GDP
    a.   federal nondefense spending is the most volatile and most directly correlated with GDP.
    b.   consumption is inversely correlated with GDP.
    c.   investment is not the most volatile but its size and direction correlation with GDP make it unusually important.
    d.   federal defense spending is the most stable.
    e.   residential construction is the most stable.

Topics for Discussion

1. From the Keynesian approach we know that increases in government spending increase income. For the quantity theory to be consistent with this, income velocity must rise as government spending increases. Why would it?

2. How do you think the baby boom of the 1950s affected consumption? The baby boomers are in their midthirties now, so should consumption be a high or a low fraction of income?

3. The Keynesian model assumes that when firms find they cannot sell all that they intended, they cut production. Do you think firms do this? Or do they cut prices or launch an advertising campaign?

4. Why do interest rates tend to rise as customers and businesses regain confidence and spend their way out of a recession?

5. Why do shifts in aggregate expenditures generate further shifts in the same direction? Try to think of both real and monetary effects.

Exercise Questions

1. *a.* Imagine an economy made up of 40 workers. Production uses only labor and there are no bosses, profit, or government. Each employed worker receives $50 a day. All workers spend $10 a day plus half of whatever they earn. What is the consumption function for this economy?

   b. The production facilities are run by a workers' committee. (This is done for simplicity.) There are 12 production lines capable of employing 4 people each for a grand total of 48 possible jobs. The workers' committee has decided to invest $400 each period. Fill in Table 15.1. Income is equal to the number of people hired times $50. Consumption is half income plus $400. Planned investment is $400. Calculate consumption plus planned investment, $C + I$. This is aggregate expenditures. Compare this to production. (Production equals income because production generates income for someone.) Now subtract demand from production, $Y - (C + I)$. This is unplanned inventory accumulation. If unplanned inventory accumulation is negative, more workers will be hired. If unplanned inventory accumulation is positive, fewer will be hired.

Table 15.1 Income, Consumption, and Employment Figures

Number hired	Income	Consumption	$C + I$	Unplanned inventory accumulation	Are more or fewer hired?
40					
36					
32					
28					
16					
0					

2. Draw the $C + I$ and 45-degree lines that correspond to the economy above in Figure 15.1. To plot the $C + I$ line, first plot the consumption and income pairs you calculated in Question 1 as the consumption function, then add $400 to this for the $C + I$ line.

Figure 15.1 The 45-Degree Diagram for the Workers' Economy

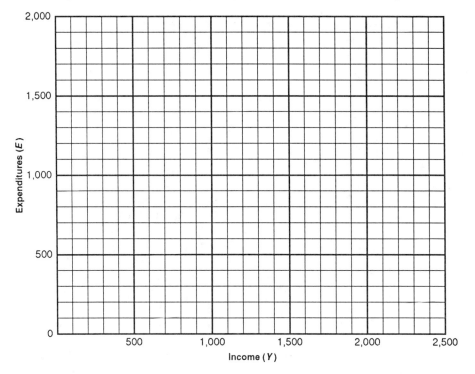

3. Confirm that the equilibrium income levels you found in Questions 1 and 2 above are correct by multiplying planned investment plus autonomous consumption by the investment multiplier.

4. Use diagrams like the one you constructed above to illustrate the effects of:
   a. higher taxes
   b. higher government spending
   c. lower investment

5. How must the changes in Question 4 change income velocity if the quantity theory and the income-expenditure approach are consistent? How do you know?

Answers to Self-Tests

Completion

1. income, the money supply
2. investment
3. disposable income
4. permanent income
5. depreciation; interest rate; risk premium; tax effect
6. net investment
7. factoring
8. net exports
9. nominal, real
10. accelerator
11. 4
12. nominal, real
13. interest rates, income, prices; prices

True-False

1. False
2. False
3. True
4. True
5. False
6. True
7. False
8. False
9. True
10. False
11. True
12. False
13. False

Multiple Choice

1. c
2. d
3. b
4. a
5. b
6. b
7. e
8. d
9. e
10. b
11. b
12. c

Answers to Exercise Questions

1. *a.* $C = .5Y + \$400.$
    b.

Answer to Table 15.1   Income, Consumption, and Employment Figures

Number hired	Income	Consumption	$C + I$	Unplanned inventory accumulation	Are more or fewer hired?
40	$2,000	$1,400	$1,800	$200	Fewer
36	1,800	1,300	1,700	100	Fewer
32	1,600	1,200	1,600	0	No change
28	1,400	1,100	1,500	−100	More
16	800	800	1,200	−400	More
0	0	400	800	−800	More

2. **Answer to Figure 15.1**   The 45-Degree Diagram for the Workers' Economy

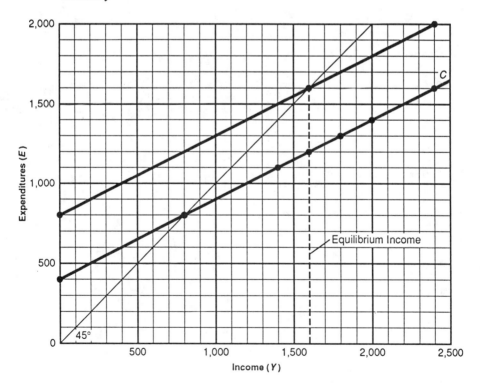

3. $(400 + 400)(1/.5) = 1,600$.

4. a. An increase in taxes reduces disposable income and consumption. Therefore the $C + I$ line shifts down and equilibrium income falls.

    b. An increase in government spending increases demand. Demand is now $C + I + G$. Equilibrium income increases.

    c. A reduction in investment reduces $C + I$ and equilibrium income falls.

5. The quantity theory equation is $MV = PY$. In the income-expenditure exercises above, P and M are assumed constant. If P and M are constant but Y changes, then V must change in the same direction as Y to preserve the equality. Parts a and c result in a lower income level, so velocity must have declined; in part b income increased, so velocity must have increased. Why velocity changes will be explained in Chapter 17.

CHAPTER 16   Aggregate Expenditures and
                 the Interest Rate

Learning Objectives

1. Explain why interest rates are important.

2. Use the loanable funds theory to explain how interest rates are determined.

3. Explain the time path of interest rates given an increase in the supply of money, and explain the sensitivity of the time path to expected inflation and price flexibility.

4. Explain how taxes and the expected inflation rate affect nominal interest rates.

Key Terms, Concepts, and Institutions

loanable funds theory
capital inflows
inflation premium
rational expectations
real interest rate
expectations effect
income and price effects
systematic errors

expected inflation rate
nominal interest rate
after-tax real interest rate
Fisher effect
adaptive expectations (error-learning
    model)
liquidity effect

Self-Test: Completion

1. The three sources of loanable funds are _____ , _____
   , and the _____ .

2. If the dollar is depreciating at 4 percent a year compared to the Japanese yen and if unrestricted Japanese securities pay 6 percent a year, then comparable U.S. securities would have to pay about

    _____ percent to compete.

3. Assuming that expectations are rational, people will not make

    _____ errors for any length of time. They will still make errors, but these errors will be random with a mean of zero.

4. The nominal interest rate can be broken into two components, the

    expected _____ of interest and expected _____ .

5. If anticipated inflation is 8 percent, the nominal interest rate is 12 percent, and the tax rate is 50 percent, then the real after-tax rate of

    interest is _____ percent.

6. An increase in the money supply may reduce nominal interest rates, at least until prices and expectations begin to adjust. This is called the

    _____ .

7. A professor is ten minutes late for the beginning of class and announces he has an immediately preceding class across campus. A

    student using _____ expectations may allow herself an additional five minutes before coming to class the next day, while a

    student using _____ expectations may take the full ten minutes.

8. If people are constantly searching for models that predict events and throw out those that lead to systematic error, then they are using a

    _____ expectations approach.

9. If announced increases in the supply of money had no impact on employment or output, and led to suddenly higher inflation and nominal interest rates, this would be evidence that the economy had

    _____ prices and _____ expectations.

10. A change in the nominal interest rate point for point with a change in

    the inflation rate is called the _____ effect.

Self-Test: True-False

1. Real savings by households exceed real savings by firms.

2. An increase in interest rates increases the supply of loanable funds because banks will hold fewer excess reserves and the money multiplier will rise.

3. An increase in the demand for money can increase the demand for loanable funds, as businesses or households borrow to acquire the additional cash.

4. An increase in foreign interest rates would shift the supply of loanable funds to the left and lead to higher interest rates at home.

5. An increase in interest rates reduces the demand for loanable funds because higher interest rates increase investment.

6. If expected inflation is 7 percent and the nominal interest rate is 10 percent, then the expected real rate of interest, ignoring potential tax effects, is 17 percent.

7. Adaptive expectations can be explained as expectations that are an average of past experience. If inflation were suddenly to increase, it would take some time before the expectation caught up with reality.

8. Higher money growth cannot lead to lower nominal interest rates except for a short time. However, the inflation created may reduce after-tax real interest rates.

9. Even if formal and informal contracts that make prices slow to adjust exist, the rational-expectations theory implies that money has no impact on real interest rates or output.

10. The way in which our tax system treats interest income means that when the inflation rate rises, the before-tax nominal interest rate should rise by less than the increase in the inflation rate.

11. For much of the 1970s, the real after-tax interest rate was negative.

12. The need for new investment in Eastern Europe, Russia, and China may not cause interest rates to rise. For example, funds could flow from Russia to the United States in search of safety.

Self-Test: Multiple Choice

1. An increase in the real money supply increases real loanable funds because
   a. a higher money supply is a reflection of higher government lending.
   b. in our system bank loan creation and money creation are intertwined.
   c. as people expect more inflation they are more willing to make loans.
   d. there is no difference between loans and money.
   e. both *a* and *b*.

2. An economics department printed up T-shirts that read: "Fast money raises my interest." This is an example of
   a. the liquidity effect.
   b. the Darby effect.
   c. the Fisher effect.
   d. an effect due to sticky prices.
   e. irrational expectations.

3. If prices are completely flexible, then an increases in the nominal money supply
   a. reduces nominal and real interest rates.
   b. increases income as the real money supply rises.
   c. reduces unemployment.
   d. leaves interest rates, investment, income, and employment unaffected as prices increase in proportion to the increase in the nominal money supply.
   e. changes the real money supply.

4. Given sticky prices, if the nominal money supply rises,
   a. the real money supply must fall.
   b. interest rates will rise as expected inflation accelerates.
   c. nominal and real interest rates fall temporarily.
   d. unemployment increases as investment declines due to lower rewards.
   e. nominal interest rates will fall permanently.

5. The demand for loanable funds increases if
   a. the budget deficit increases.
   b. households save more.
   c. the money supply increases.
   d. firms reduce investment.
   e. banks hold fewer excess reserves.

6. The supply of loanable funds increases if
   a. interest rates in Japan or Germany increase.
   b. the budget deficit increases.
   c. households save more.
   d. firms reduce investment.
   e. the Fed sells government securities.

7. If the Fed were to buy government securities on the open market, we
   would expect the supply of loanable funds to _____ , the supply
   of money to _____ , and the interest rate to _____ .
   a. increase, increase, increase
   b. increase, increase, decrease
   c. decrease, increase, decrease
   d. decrease, decrease, increase
   e. increase, decrease, increase

8. If the money supply rises in a completely price flexible economy, then
   output and employment _____ , prices _____ , and the
   real money supply _____ .
   a. increase, increase, increases
   b. do not change, increase, increases
   c. do not change, increase, does not change
   d. increase, increase, decreases
   e. increase, increase, does not change

9. If expectations are adaptive and prices are slow to adjust, then an
   increase in the supply of money will, for a limited time, _____
   the expected real interest rate, _____ employment and output,
   and _____ the real money supply.
   a. increase, increase, increase
   b. not change, increase, increase
   c. not change, increase, not change
   d. decrease, increase, increase
   e. decrease, increase, not change

10. Inflation can affect the real interest rate because
    a. inflation increases uncertainty and thereby increases savings and
       reduces investment.
    b. inflation increases wealth so people save less.
    c. inflation reduces the corporate tax burden.

    d. assuming flexible prices, inflation increases income and leads to higher investment through an accelerator effect.

    e. all the above.

11. If you become aware that the Fed is about to enter the market and buy bonds aggressively and if

    a. this leads to higher expected inflation, then interest rates must fall.

    b. expected inflation does not change, then interest rates must fall.

    c. the move is to counter a sale of bonds by the Treasury, interest rates will rise.

    d. the move was anticipated by the market, then interest rates may not change at all.

    e. the news attracts foreign capital, then interest rates will rise.

Topics for Discussion

1. According to the error-learning model of expectations, the public estimates inflation by looking only at historical data. But according to rational-expectations theory, people forecast in a rational way, using all information available to them. What other information might people take into account when forming their expectations about inflation?

2. You will find "Credit Markets" as a "Today's Contents" heading on the bottom of the first page of today's *Wall Street Journal*. Turn to the page indicated and interpret the day's events with either the loanable funds or liquidity preference theory.

3. The text discusses the effects of an increase in monetary growth. What would happen to the time path of interest rates, output, and inflation if the Fed reduced monetary growth? How does this compare with the U.S. economy in the early 1990s? (See the endpapers of the text.)

Exercise Questions

1. The main point of the chapter is to develop some sense of what happens as the money supply rises. The problem is that economists are somewhat divided over both the degree of price flexibility and the rationality of expectations. These disagreements are at least part of the reason for the large number of cases discussed. Circle the appropriate options in the paragraph below to summarize the main effects of an increase in the money supply under different assumptions.

    As the Fed buys bonds to increase the money supply, the interest on bonds must (*a*: rise/fall) because buying bonds increases the (*b*: supply of/demand for) loanable funds. The change in interest rates (*c*:

increases/reduces) investment by firms in plant and equipment and is a (*d*: shift in/movement along) the demand for loanable funds. The change in investment leads to (*e*: an increase/a decrease) in employment. The higher employment and income leads to (*f*: higher/lower) money demand and (*g*: higher/lower) prices of goods. Both effects tend to (*h*: raise/lower) the rate of interest. If prices are relatively flexible and people understand the effect of money on prices, then the decline in interest rates lasts for a relatively (*i*: longer/shorter) period. In the limit of perfect price flexibility, the real money supply and the real interest rate (*j*: increase/decrease/don't change at all).

2. The fall of 1992 produced very large exchange-rate realignments between Germany and the United Kingdom. During the unification of East and West Germany, the German money supply increased rapidly, and this pushed inflation up from 2 to 4 percent. The Bundesbank (the German central bank) responded in the fall of 1992 by restricting money growth and increasing interest rates. Meanwhile, in England a prolonged recession and slow money growth had succeeded in bringing inflation down from over 10 percent in 1990 to 4 percent in 1992. The sudden change in Bundesbank policy forced England to choose between even tighter money and higher interest rates or a rapidly declining value of the pound. The pound fell dramatically; this highlighted the problems of the planned monetary union. How does this illustrate concepts presented in the chapter?

3. On June 5, 1995, the *Wall Street Journal* reported (p. C1), "Alan Greenspan may not see a recession on the horizon, but it sure looks as if a few people in the bond market do." What happened to bond prices and yields?

4. There have been several articles recently noting that baby boomers and their offspring continue to save very little. What are some predictable consequences in the loanable funds market of low household savings rates?

Answers to Self-Tests

Completion

1. savings, capital inflow, money supply
2. 10
3. systematic
4. real rate, inflation
5. −2
6. liquidity effect
7. adaptive, rational
8. rational
9. flexible, rational
10. Fisher

True-False

1.	False	7.	True
2.	True	8.	True
3.	True	9.	False
4.	True	10.	False
5.	False	11.	True
6.	False	12.	True

Multiple Choice

1.	b	7.	b
2.	c	8.	c
3.	d	9.	d
4.	c	10.	a
5.	a	11.	d
6.	c		

Answers to Exercise Questions

1.
   a. fall
   b. supply
   c. increases
   d. movement along
   e. an increase
   f. higher
   g. higher
   h. raise
   i. shorter
   j. don't change at all

2. The British became painfully aware that prices are not perfectly flexible and that capital flows between countries in search of high yields are massive and rapid with immediate effects on the exchange rate. The German experience supports the proposition that inflation responds to money growth with a time lag.

3. The expected slowdown in income growth led to predictions that the demand for loanable funds would decline and interest rates would fall. Lower interest rates are higher bond prices and there was a strong bond rally. The expected decline in employment also caused people to revise their inflation forecasts downward; this led to lower nominal interest rates.

4. Lower savings by households reduce the supply of loanable funds and this leads, if nothing else changes, to higher real domestic interest rates. But, given that we live in a world capital market, we would expect this to continue to attract an inflow of foreign capital. Borrowing from abroad should allow us to continue to import more than we export. The inflow of foreign capital is beneficial in the sense that it allows lower

interest rates and higher investment, but large foreign debts do make the U.S. economy increasingly sensitive to the continued trust and confidence of foreign investors. Given that household savings tend to flow toward banks, the weak saving is also bad news for bankers.

CHAPTER 17   Aggregate Expenditures and the Demand for Money

Learning Objectives

1. State the connection between the demand for money and the interest rate.

2. Differentiate between transactions, savings, and precautionary demands for money.

3. Explain why both the interest rate and the cost of investing affect the transactions demand for money.

4. Explain why the interest rate and the cost of selling assets affect the precautionary demand for money.

5. Explain how the gap between the interest rate paid on deposits and the rates on alternative stores of saving affect the savings demand for money.

6. Apply standard demand theory to the demand for money.

7. Explain why estimated money demand functions failed to predict actual demand well into the 1970s and early 1980s.

Key Terms, Concepts, and Institutions

transactions demand
net interest forgone
complements
the case of the missing money
precautionary demand

cost of investing
substitutes
demand function
statistical demand function
savings demand for money

Self-Test: Completion

1. If the public holds large volumes of Treasury bills and money-market accounts, the cost of selling assets will be low. These are examples of

   _____ assets.

2. Someone who converts all her monthly income to cash and spends it gradually over the month may be ignoring the potential benefits of

   _____ .

3. Money held in the event of an unforeseen expense is called a

   _____ demand for money.

4. Money held to meet anticipated expenses is called a _____ demand for money.

5. In general, the demand for a good depends on its own price, the prices

   of _____ , and the prices of _____ .

6. In general, demand depends not only on prices but also on

   _____ and _____ .

7. If the demand for money were to increase because people were more confident about the future, we would say demand shifted due to a

   change in _____ . (List one of the determinants of money demand.)

8. An increase in anticipated stock returns would shift money demand

   through a change in _____ . (List one of the determinants of money demand.)

9. Payment of interest on checkable deposits changed the amount of

   money demanded by changing _____ . (List one of the determinants of money demand.)

10. The main explanation for the overestimation of money demand in the

    1970s was _____ .

11. Holders of _____ money balances are much more likely to

    invest their money balances than are holders of _____ .

Self-Test: True-False

1. $M\text{-}1$ velocity grows at a stable rate.

2.   The higher the cost of investing and later disinvesting, the lower monetary holdings will be.

3.   The trouble involved in acquiring and later liquidating securities rises in proportion to the amount involved.

4.   The marginal benefit of precautionary balances decreases as more precautionary balances are held.

5.   The savings demand for money depends on the gap between the interest rate paid on deposits and the rates on alternative stores of savings.

6.   In general we think that an increase in the price of a substitute good should increase the demand for a good.

7.   A credit card is a complement to money.

8.   Changes in payments habits change money demand through the taste variable.

9.   The failure of the demand-for-money functions in the 1980s is partly due to new regulations that allow checkable deposits to pay interest.

10.   Savings demand is more interest elastic than transactions demand.

Self-Test: Multiple Choice

1.   When economists say someone has an excess supply of money, they
     a.   are making a joke—no one has more money than he or she wants.
     b.   means that the person would rather have some good, service, or asset than the excess money he or she currently holds.
     c.   means the person is holding money for a possible need that probably will not arise.
     d.   means the person is holding money in the hope interest rates will rise and bond prices fall.
     e.   either *c* or *d.*

2.   Precautionary balances would rise if
     a.   anticipated expenses rose.
     b.   unemployment, and therefore uncertainty, increased.
     c.   interest rates became more stable so that potential capital gains declined.

    d. people are holding a large volume of liquid assets like Treasury securities.

    e. bond interest rates rose.

3. The benefit of holding a precautionary balance is that it avoids the cost of
    a. cutting planned expenditures.
    b. forced liquidation of an asset.
    c. borrowing.
    d. defaulting on an obligation.
    e. the least cost combination of the above.

4. The size of the precautionary balance is optimal if for a net interest cost of 6 percent and a borrowing cost of 18 percent, the probability that the last dollar of the precautionary balance will be used is
    a. 108 percent.
    b. 1 percent.
    c. 33.33 percent.
    d. 12 percent.
    e. 24 percent.

5. If income increases,
    a. the demand for money will increase.
    b. the supply of money will increase.
    c. the supply of money will decrease.
    d. interest rates will fall.
    e. interest velocity will fall.

6. The dominant explanation for the large errors in the statistical money demand equations is that
    a. inflation created uncertainty and large fluctuations in precautionary demand.
    b. more people became adept at playing the bond market so that investor optimism and pessimism had a larger influence on money demand
    c. more people were paid cash bonuses based on performance; that altered payments patterns and increased uncertainty.
    d. the OPEC price increases forced people to economize on cash holdings to an unanticipated degree.
    e. the higher interest rates and lower data-processing costs led to rapid financial innovation.

7. Statistical money demand functions generally include
    a. prices of complements.
    b. prices of substitutes.

    c.   tastes.
    d.   the costs of investing.
    e.   a short-term interest rate.

8. If it were possible costlessly and instantaneously to convert high-interest bonds to low-interest money, then the demand for money would be
    a.   zero.
    b.   equal to monthly income.
    c.   higher the higher the bond rate of interest.
    d.   lower the higher the bond rate of interest.
    e.   equal to precautionary plus speculative demand, and transactions demand would be zero.

9. The transactions demand for money increases if
    a.   people convert bonds to cash more frequently due to low conversion fees.
    b.   the bond rate of interest increases.
    c.   income increases.
    d.   people expect bond interest rates to decline.
    e.   the reduction of health care benefits increases uncertainty.

10. If the bond rate of interest increases, then the transactions demand for money _____ , while the precautionary demand for money

_____ .
    a.   increases, increases
    b.   increases, decreases
    c.   increases, does not change
    d.   decreases, increases
    e.   decreases, decreases

11. Comparing *M-1, M-2,* and *M-3,* the demand for _____ has been least stable, while the Fed can control _____ best.
    a.   *M-1, M-3*
    b.   *M-2, M-3*
    c.   *M-2, M-2*
    d.   *M-3, M-1*
    e.   *M-1, M-1*

12. Which of the following decreases the demand for precautionary balances?
    a.   The probability of having to make unanticipated payments increases.
    b.   Households and firms decrease their holdings of liquid assets.
    c.   The net interest rate falls.

d. Interest rates fluctuate less.

e. The interest rate at which firms can borrow increases.

Topics for Discussion

1. Keynesians sometimes argue that money demand reflects business expectations. If you anticipate low yields in business, hold more money. In this scenario, the business fluctuation causes the change in money demand—not the other way around. Is the quantity theory a useful device if such reverse causation is common? Is the remarkably steady growth of velocity, at least well into the 1980s, consistent with the scenario?

2. Milton Friedman has long complained that the case of the missing money and similar episodes are not evidence of an unstable money demand. He believes the episodes simply demonstrate the inadequacy of the bad statistical money demand functions traditionally used by economists. Compare the standard demand theory with the components of a statistical money demand function. Do you agree with Friedman? Where does this leave the Fed? Do they have an alternative to relying on the bad(?) functions economists use for fit?

Exercise Questions

1. Indicate whether money demand will rise or fall for each shock listed below, and indicate whether this is an example of a transactions, precautionary, or savings demand.
   a. The minimum denomination of Treasury bills is increased.
   b. It is December and Christmas is in the air.
   c. The cost and inconvenience of investing in securities or near-monies increases.
   d. An aging population nears retirement.
   e. A recession increases the probability of workers' being laid off.
   f. Interest rates become more volatile so that the prices of bonds and securities become less certain.

2. For each variable listed below, state whether it is included in the theoretical and/or statistical money demand function. If it is included in one but not the other, explain why.
   a. income
   b. money complements
   c. payments technology
   d. price level
   e. anticipated stock return

  f. short-term interest rate
  g. permanent income
  h. wire transfers

3. Match the terms below with the appropriate statement:
Transaction demand for money
Precautionary demand for money
Savings demand for money
  a. These balances are held for unexpected expenditures.
  b. The demand for these balances is positively related to the volume of planned transactions.
  c. These balances depend on the gap between the interest rate paid on deposits and the rates available on alternative stores of savings, like securities.

4. . . . Kurt Karl, head of macroeconomic forecasting for the WEFA Group in suburban Philadelphia . . . said that if the Fed doesn't raise rates at its next meeting at the end of this month, 'they will definitely do it at the meeting in June.' *Wall Street Journal,* March 13, 1995, p. A2.

If the Fed does raise interest rates, people will want to hold _____ (more/less) money balances.

Answers to Self-Tests

Completion

1. liquid
2. investing
3. precautionary
4. transactions
5. substitutes, complements
6. income, tastes
7. tastes
8. the price of a substitute
9. money's own price
10. financial innovation
11. large, small

True-False

1. False
2. False
3. False
4. True
5. True
6. True
7. False
8. True
9. True
10. True

Multiple Choice

1.	*b*	7.	*e*
2.	*b*	8.	*a*
3.	*e*	9.	*c*
4.	*c*	10.	*e*
5.	*a*	11.	*e*
6.	*e*	12.	*d*

Answers to Exercise Questions

1. All the shocks listed increase money demand.
   - *a.* savings
   - *b.* transactions
   - *c.* transactions
   - *d.* savings
   - *e.* precautionary
   - *f.* precautionary

2. *a.* Both.
   - *b.* Neither.
   - *c.* Theoretical only; no good measure of technology exists.
   - *d.* Both.
   - *e.* Theoretical and a very few statistical functions; measuring anticipated returns is difficult.
   - *f.* Both.
   - *g.* Theoretical and some statistical functions.
   - *h.* Statistical only: it works, but no one knows why. It may be closely related to some of the variables that belong in money demand that we can't measure.

3. *a.* precautionary demand for money
   - *b.* transactions demand for money
   - *c.* savings demand for money

4. less

CHAPTER 18   Aggregate Expenditures: The Complete Model

Learning Objectives

1. Explain the factors that determine the slopes of the IS and LM curves.

2. Explain the factors that cause shifts of the IS and LM curves.

3. Use the IS-LM model to illustrate the effects of changing consumption, investment, taxes, government spending, money supply, and money demand on interest rates and income.

4. Explain how an increase in government spending can crowd out private investment through higher interest rates and crowd out production by reducing net exports.

5. Explain how bond-financed government spending could shift the LM curve (this could accentuate or reduce the crowding-out effect).

6. Explain crowding in.

7. Explain how fiscal and monetary policies affect income and interest rates using the IS-LM framework.

7. Cite criticisms of the IS-LM framework.

Key Terms, Concepts, and Institutions

money market
simultaneous equilibrium
LM curve
expenditures slope
interest inelasticity
IS-LM diagram

crowding in
goods and services market
IS curve
crowding out
portfolio crowding out
market equilibrium curve

Self-Test: Completion

1. The collection of interest income pairs where the demand for and supply of goods and services are equal is called the _____ .

2. The collection of interest income pairs where the demand for and supply of money are equal is called the _____ .

3. The LM curve is steep if money demand is more responsive to changes in _____ than _____ .

4. The slope of the IS curve becomes flatter if the multiplier _____ .

5. In this chapter the _____ refers to the total cost and difficulty of borrowing.

6. While the interest rate probably affects all the components of income $(C + I + G + X)$, the effect on _____ is least certain.

7. The LM curve is not a supply curve or a demand curve but a _____ curve.

8. An interest income pair below both the IS and LM curves indicates excess _____ (supply or demand) in the money market and excess _____ (supply or demand) in the goods market.

9. As the supply of securities increases—and their prices decline—the demand for money will rise if money and securities are _____ .

10. Crowding in could occur if money and securities were _____ .

Self-Test: True-False

1. At an interest income pair above the IS curve, demand is less than production, unplanned inventories are accumulating, and businesses will cut back output.

2. At an interest income pair above the LM curve, money demand is greater than money supply and people will sell bonds in an attempt to acquire the money they want; this forces the interest rate higher.

3. If near-monies develop, the LM curve will shift toward lower interest rates and higher income.

4. If interest rates increase, investments increase because investments earn more.

5. Changes in money supply or money demand shift the LM curve, while changes in $C + I + G + X$ shift the IS curve as long as the changes are not caused by a change in bond interest rates or income. (Such changes are reflected in the slopes of the curves.)

6. Higher interest rates reduce investment. Therefore, whenever interest rates rise, the IS curve shifts toward lower income.

7. Higher income increases the demand for money. Therefore, whenever income rises, the LM curve shifts toward higher interest rates.

8. An increase in consumer confidence increases spending and therefore shifts the IS curve toward higher income.

9. Paying interest on checkable deposits increases the demand for money, but since the change is induced by interest rates, the LM curve does not shift. (Remember that this happened in 1980.)

10. If the Fed kept the interest rate constant as G increased, then according to the IS-LM model, income would rise by G times the multiplier.

Self-Test: Multiple Choice

1. If money demand were to increase, interest rates would tend to _____ .
   This can be represented by shifting the LM curve _____ .
   a. fall; up
   b. fall; down
   c. rise; up
   d. rise; down

2. If the LM curve shifts up, the change in interest rates causes investment
   to _____ and output to _____ .
   a. rise, rise
   b. rise, fall
   c. fall, rise
   d. fall, fall

3. An increase in taxes shifts the
   a. IS curve up.
   b. IS curve down.
   c. LM curve up.
   d. LM curve down.

4. A tax increase leads to a _____ interest rate and _____ income.
   a. lower, lower
   b. lower, higher
   c. higher, lower
   d. higher, higher

5. Assume investors suddenly become nervous about the future and reduce investment at every interest rate. This would shift the
   a. IS curve up.
   b. IS curve down.
   c. LM curve up.
   d. LM curve down.

6. Continuing Question 5, the effect of investor panic is _____

   interest rates and _____ income.
   a. lower, lower
   b. lower, higher
   c. higher, lower
   d. higher, higher

7. The IS curve is downward sloping in part because
   a. higher prices reduce the demand for goods.
   b. higher income increases money demand and interest rates.
   c. lower interest rates stimulate investment and increase income.
   d. lower interest rates reduce profit, investment, and income.
   e. higher interest rates lead to a higher dollar value and increase our income.

8. The LM curve is upward sloping because
   a. higher prices increase money demand and interest rates.
   b. higher interest rates here increase foreign demand for the dollar, so our income rises.
   c. higher interest rates increase the demand for money and income.
   d. lower interest rates stimulate investment and increase income.
   e. higher income increases money demand and this increases interest rates.

9. The IS curve is steep if expenditures are _____ to the interest

   rate and the multiplier is _____ .
   a. sensitive, large
   b. sensitive, small
   c. insensitive, large
   d. insensitive, small

10. Portfolio crowding out results if
   a.   people consider the future tax burden in current spending policies.
   b.   people consider government bonds a money substitute so that an increase in bond wealth reduces money demand.
   c.   people consider government bonds a money complement so that an increase in bond wealth increases money demand.
   d.   higher interest rates increase the value of the dollar.
   e.   people ignore the future tax burden in current spending policies.

Topics for Discussion

1.   Before 1972, the value of the dollar did not vary directly with interest rates because of a treaty signed in 1944 that controlled exchange rates. By the mid-1970s the treaty collapsed. How do you think the emergence of a direct interest rate–exchange rate link affected the expenditure slope and crowding out?

2.   Find some economic forecasts that discuss interest rates and income. Monday's outlook column of the *Wall Street Journal* will do nicely. Are the effects the *Journal* discusses included in the IS-LM model? Are the effects discussed in the article that are not part of the IS-LM model significant or insignificant?

3.   Does the IS-LM model adequately discuss
   a.   tax reform?
   b.   oil price changes?
   c.   changes in expected inflation?
   d.   popular reaction to announced policies?
   e.   changes in expected output?
   f.   the time needed for changes to be apparent in income?

Exercise Questions

1.   In this exercise you will construct and use an IS-LM diagram for an imaginary economy. In this economy the consumption function is $400 + .5Y$.

   a.   What is the marginal propensity to consume?

   b.   What is the multiplier?

   c.   As the bond rate of interest rises, the desired level of investment falls because the higher interest rate represents a higher borrowing cost. This is reflected in Table 18.1. Fill in the blanks of the table.

Autonomous spending is desired investment plus the autonomous part of consumption, in this case $400. Recall that the multiplier times autonomous spending equals equilibrium income.

Table 18.1

Interest rate	Desired investment	Autonomous spending	×	The multiplier	=	Equilibrium income
5	$600					
10	400					
15	200					

These interest rate and income pairs are three points on this economy's IS curve. Plot these points on Figure 18.1.

Figure 18.1   The Workers' IS-LM Diagram

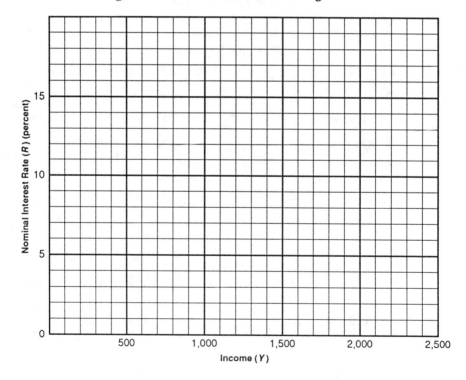

2. The money demand function for this economy is

$M_d = .5Y - 40R.$

Money supply is equal to $400. Find the income levels where the money supply equals money demand for the interest rates listed in Table 18.2.

Table 18.2 Equilibrium Points for the LM Curve

Nominal interest rate (R)	Income (Y)
15%	$_____(a)
10	_____(b)
5	_____(c)

The numbers in Table 18.2 are points on the LM curve. Plot them on Figure 18.1. The workers' committee has two ways it could achieve full employment. It could form a government to increase production, or it could increase the money stock. We can now calculate how much of each would be required. Full employment occurs at an income level of $2,000. To maintain this output level, the workers' committee must

invest (d: $_____), which they will not do unless the interest

rate is (e: _____). At this interest and income combination the

money demand is (f: $_____). To reach this level, the money

stock must be raised by (g: $_____). On Figure 18.1, draw the LM curve for this money stock and label it LM' (you just found one point and LM' is parallel to LM through this point).

3. Alternatively, the workers' committee could sell bonds and use the proceeds to finance public works. At an income level of $2,000 and a money supply of $400, we know the interest rate will be

(a: _____) and the workers' committee will invest only

(b: $_____). On the basis of the formula that appears in Table 18.1,

we need (400 + 200 + G)(2) = $2,000. G needs to be (c: $_____). On Figure 18.1, draw the IS curve for this government spending level and label it IS' (you have just calculated one point and IS' is parallel to IS through this point).

4. In March of 1995, Kurt Karl, head of macroeconomic forecasting for the WEFA Group in suburban Philadelphia, expected the Fed to raise interest rates in June of that year (*Wall Street Journal*, March 13, 1995, p. A2). Use

the IS-LM diagram below to show the effects of this expected change in monetary policy.

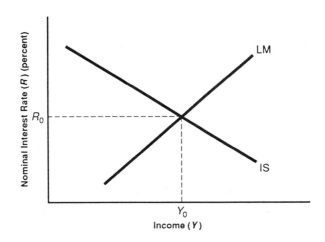

Nominal income would (increase/decrease). Mr. Karl thinks the Fed would make this move to combat (inflation/unemployment).

Answers to Self-Tests

Completion

1. IS curve
2. LM curve
3. income, interest rate
4. increases
5. interest rate

6. government spending
7. market equilibrium
8. demand, demand
9. complements
10. substitutes

True-False

1. True
2. False
3. True
4. False
5. True

6. False
7. False
8. True
9. False
10. True

Multiple Choice

1.	*c*	6.	*a*
2.	*d*	7.	*c*
3.	*b*	8.	*e*
4.	*a*	9.	*d*
5.	*b*	10.	*c*

Answers to Exercise Questions

1. *a.* .5
   b. 2
   c.

Table 18.1

Interest rate	Desired investment	Autonomous spending	×	The multiplier	=	Equilibrium income
5	$600	$1,000		2		$2,000
10	400	800		2		1,600
15	200	600		2		1,200

Answer to Figure 18.1   The Workers' IS-LM Diagram

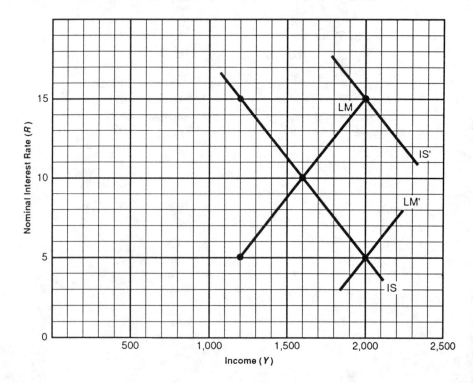

2. *a.* 2,000
    b. 1,600
    c. 1,200
    d. 600
    e. 5 percent
    f. $800
    g. $400

3. *a.* 15 percent
    b. 200
    c. $400

4.

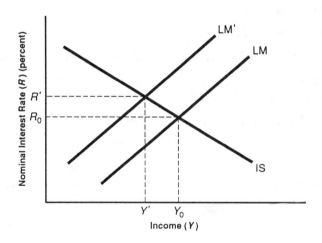

decrease; inflation

CHAPTER 19   Inflation and Unemployment

Learning Objectives

1. State the implications of the Phillips curve and the expectations-augmented Phillips curve.

2. Explain the concept of the NAIRU.

3. Explain the slopes of the aggregate demand and aggregate supply curves.

4. Give examples of demand- and supply shocks, and explain why these shocks are not likely to cause persistent inflation.

5. State the advantages and disadvantages of the various policies to fight inflation.

6. Cite causes of unemployment.

7. Explain why a major inflation requires an increase in the money stock.

8. Define inflation and unemployment.

Key Terms, Concepts, and Institutions

inflation
hyperinflation
consumer price index
unemployment
frictional unemployment
short-run Phillips curve
expectations-augmented
   Phillips curve
indexing
hysteresis
cost-push inflation
price-wage-price spiral

natural rate of unemployment
   (NAIRU)
aggregate demand
aggregate supply curve
supply shocks
demand shocks
incomes policy
jawboning
social contract
demand-pull inflation
COLA
sacrifice ratio

Self-Test: Completion

1. _____ unemployment is needed for an efficient economy.

2. The rate of inflation associated with any given output level will be _____ as productivity declines.

3. The _____ becomes a vertical line at the NAIRU when people correctly anticipate the inflation rate.

4. The unemployment rate that is just high enough to avoid ever accelerating inflation is called the _____ .

5. The _____ relates the price level to output.

6. Elimination of minimum wage laws and programs to retrain the unemployed might _____ the NAIRU.

7. Stabilization policies tend to _____ the effects of anti-inflation measures.

8. The Phillips curve relates the rate of _____ to the rate of _____ .

9. Pervasive crop failures would be an example of a _____ shock.

10. According to the text, incomes policies have three defects. First, jawboning may be _____ . Second, _____ distort resource allocation. Third, with controls in place it is tempting to continue with _____ macro policies.

11. A situation in which the previous value of a variable has a significant effect on its current value is called _____ .

12. Cost-push inflations may be caused by _____ shocks.

13. The cost in forgone output of reducing the inflation rate by 1 percentage point is known as the _____ .

Self-Test: True-False

1. An increase in the demand for money will cause the aggregate demand curve to shift upward.

2. The most likely cause for a major inflation is an increase in the money stock.

3. Other things being equal, wages increase faster when unemployment is low.

4. No steady rate of inflation is possible if the unemployment rate is below NAIRU.

5. A rise in unemployment may be due to an increase in the marginal efficiency of investment.

6. A one-time rise in the interest rate increases aggregate demand and may account for prolonged inflation.

7. An increase in aggregate demand initially causes output and prices to rise.

8. The short-run Phillips curve suggests a positive relationship between inflation and unemployment.

9. An increase in oil prices must, in the long run, increase the price level.

10. Claiming that monetary growth causes inflation without explaining monetary growth is superficial.

11. Most economists advocate fighting inflation as opposed to fighting unemployment because they believe the sacrifice ratio is lower.

Self-Test: Multiple Choice

1. Changes in price are related _____ to changes in productivity and _____ to changes in wages.
    a. negatively, negatively
    b. negatively, positively
    c. positively, positively
    d. positively, negatively
    e. directly, inversely

2. Which of the following might cause a *decrease* in aggregate demand?
    a. an increase in government spending
    b. a reduction in taxes
    c. a reduction in the money supply
    d. an increase in the money supply
    e. *a, b,* and *d.*

3. Other things being equal, an increase in aggregate demand will
   a. reduce employment.
   b. reduce output.
   c. lower prices
   d. raise prices
   e. increase the real money supply.

4. the following are examples of supply shocks *except*
   a. a decrease in the marginal propensity to consume.
   b. rising labor costs.
   c. an increase in import prices.
   d. an increase in taxes.
   e. *a* and *d*.
   f. *b* and *c*.

5. An upward shift in aggregate supply
   a. lowers prices.
   b. raises employment.
   c. decreases employment
   d. increases the real money supply.
   e. increases output.

6. All the following are supply shocks *except*
   a. a foreign cartel's increasing import prices.
   b. widespread bad harvests.
   c. an increase in the money stock.
   d. rising labor costs due to increasing union power.
   e. increased markups resulting from a decline in competition.

7. NAIRU rose substantially in the 1970s for all of the following reasons *except*
   a. more women entering the labor force.
   b. the tendency of teenagers to change jobs frequently.
   c. the entrance of teenage baby boomers into the job market.
   d. a decrease in racial discrimination.
   e. none of the above; all are factors that account for the increase in NAIRU in the 1970s.

8. Which of the following would increase prices?
   a. a decrease in the marginal efficiency of investment
   b. an increase in the money stock
   c. a decrease in import prices
   d. an increase in aggregate supply
   e. none of the above

9. U.S. inflation history can be summarized by the following statement:
    a. Prices fell during wars and rose in peacetime.
    b. Prices rose rapidly in wars and fell gradually in peace, which continues today.
    c. Prices rose rapidly in wars and fell gradually in peace until the mid-1940s. Now prices seem to rise always.
    d. Prices rose rapidly in Democratic administrations and fell in Republican.
    e. Prices rose rapidly before the Federal Reserve System was created but have been more stable since 1917.

10. Who of the following would be considered unemployed?
    a. a nuclear physicist working part-time at McDonalds
    b. a lumberjack with a broken arm who does not look for work because he knows he will not be hired until his arm heals
    c. a healthy lumberjack who does not look for work because none of the mills in the area are buying more lumber
    d. a spoiled, unskilled teenager who is looking for work, but refuses to accept less than $40,000 a year and only wants to work 30 hours a week
    e. illegal aliens, who, whatever their job status, studiously avoid anything official—from census takers to surveys

11. Which of the following is a benefit of unemployment?
    a. There are no benefits.
    b. Unemployed people spend less; this reduces demand and inflation.
    c. Unemployed people put pressure on those with jobs to work harder and demand less pay.
    d. Unemployed people are in effect an inventory of workers available to employers. Spare parts are beneficial even if not used.
    e. *b, c,* and *d* are benefits, although it is obvious that the benefits and costs are not distributed equally.

12. Aggregate demand is downward sloping because as prices rise the
    a. real money supply increases.
    b. real money supply decreases, so wealth decreases and consumption increases.
    c. real money supply decreases, so real interest rates decrease.
    d. real money supply decreases, bond interest rates increase, and investment tends to fall.
    e. reduction in the real money supply increases bond interest rates and investment rises.

13. In the expression $w = a - bu + cq + fp^e$,
    a. q stands for unemployment.
    b. f should be greater than 1.
    c. q is the rate of productivity increase.
    d. b measures the percentage of productivity increase passed on in higher wages.
    e. expected inflation has no impact on wage demands.

Topics for Discussion

1. The *Wall Street Journal* reported on October 2, 1986, that "a longshoremen's strike shut ports from Maine to Virginia, catching shippers by surprise and threatening long-term damage to the Northeast ports." Discuss the effects of this action on aggregate expenditure, aggregate supply, the price level, and output.

2. Some argue that hyperinflations are easier to halt because in such desperate situations the government may finally be convinced that a strict anti-inflation policy is necessary and the populace may believe the government is sincere. Do you agree?

Exercise Questions

1. Suppose the administration embarks on a campaign to lower inflation by decreasing government spending and decreasing the money supply. On Figure 19.1, show how these policies will affect aggregate demand and/or long-run aggregate supply.

Figure 19.1 Aggregate Demand and Long-Run Aggregate Supply

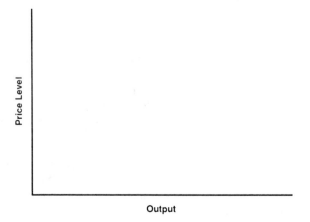

2. How do each of the following increase the level of inflation?

   a. tariffs, quotas, and voluntary restraints, such as the efforts to restrain Japanese auto imports

   b. the value of the dollar's falling on the foreign-exchange market

   c. drought in the Midwest

   d. factories operating at rates higher than their optimal capacity

   e. increasing demands by unions as unemployment decreases

3. Explain each of the following real events, using the material in the chapter.

   a. From 1963 to 1969 inflation rates increased and unemployment fell from 5.5 to 3.4 percent.

   b. From 1969 to 1970 inflation continued to rise, but unemployment rose to 4.8 percent.

   c. In 1986 the OPEC cartel experienced difficulties maintaining prices, and the consumer price index rose by only 1.1 percent.

   d. While unemployment rates in the 5 to 6 percent range generally were associated with declining inflation in the 1950s, by the late 1970s the same unemployment rates were associated with increasing inflation rates.

   e. From 1980 to 1985 inflation, as measured by the CPI, declined from 12.5 to 3.8 percent while unemployment rose from 7 percent in 1980 to a peak of 9.5 percent in 1983 and then fell to 7.1 percent in 1985.

   f. Saddam Hussein's 1990 invasion of Kuwait created fears of reduced oil supplies. Consumer confidence and sales of new homes decreased.

4. Are too many Americans at work these days for the economy's own good? Absolutely, says Martin Feldstein, a Harvard University professor and former head of the Council of Economic Advisers under President Reagan. . . . Nonsense, retorts Dana Mead, chairman and chief executive of Tenneco Inc., in Houston . . . *Wall Street Journal,* January 24, 1995, p. A1.

   a. Mr. Feldstein believes that unemployment (has fallen below/is still above) the Non-Accelerating-Inflation Rate of Unemployment, while Mr. Mead believes unemployment (has fallen below/is still above) NAIRU.

b.   . . . As the economy continues heating up, so too does the battle between the ivied halls [Feldstein] and the factory floor [Mead]. On one side, the weapon is economic theory. On the other, day-to-day experience. Much hangs in the balance:

If theory bears out, the Federal Reserve Board courts inflation if it keeps interest rates too (high/low); if many businesses' observations are correct, the Fed risks choking off economic expansion by (raising rates too high/keeping rates too low).

. . . What's more, once . . . inflation is embedded in the economy, it won't go away on it's own, these theorists maintain. Instead, the theory holds that only a period of high unemployment will help. The rough economic rule of thumb: If unemployment stays below the natural rate for two years, it will cause a permanent one-point rise in the inflation rate— that only two years of unemployment one point above the natural rate will root out . . . *Wall Street Journal,* January 24, 1995, p. A6.

c.   Besides looking at higher unemployment as a cost of bringing down inflation, economists also look at the cost in terms of forgone output to reduce inflation by 1 percentage point. According to the text, the rough economic rule of thumb would be: To reduce the inflation rate by 1 percent, the economy must lose _____ percent of one year's output, though this cost can be spread over several years. This ratio is called the _____ ratio. What does Milton Friedman, a father of NAIRU, have to say about the debate over whether the current unemployment rate is above or below NAIRU? "I don't know what the natural rate is, neither do you, and neither does anyone else. I don't try to forecast short-term changes in the economy," he says. "The record of economists in doing that justifies only humility," *Wall Street Journal,* January 14, 1995.

Answers to Self-Tests

Completion

1.   Frictional
2.   higher
3.   expectations-augmented Phillips curve
4.   NAIRU, or the natural rate of unemployment
5.   aggregate supply curve
6.   lower
7.   weaken
8.   wage (price) increases, unemployment
9.   supply
10.   ineffective; wage and price controls; expansionary

11. hysteresis
12. supply
13. sacrifice ratio

True-False

1.	False	7.	True
2.	True	8.	False
3.	True	9.	False
4.	False	10.	False
5.	False	11.	False
6.	False		

Multiple-Choice

1.	b	8.	b
2.	c	9.	c
3.	d	10.	d
4.	e	11.	e
5.	c	12.	d
6.	c	13.	c
7.	d		

Answers to Exercise Questions

1. **Answer to Figure 19.1**   Aggregate Demand and Long-Run Aggregate Supply

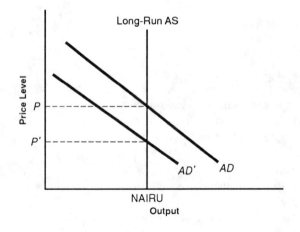

Decreasing government spending and decreasing the money supply decrease aggregate demand and do not change NAIRU; this lowers the level of prices with no change in output in the long run.

2. *a.* Supply is curtailed and prices rise, not only for imported goods but for competing goods as well.
    b. The prices of imported goods will rise.
    c. The supply of basic grains, etc., is reduced, and so prices rise.
    d. After this point, productivity tends to decline because factories are using marginal equipment, overtime shifts, and other more costly production methods. A decrease in productivity increases prices.
    e. An increase in wages without a corresponding increase in production increases prices.

3. *a.* The Vietnam War and Great Society programs boosted aggregate demand with the usual result of higher inflation and reduced unemployment.
    b. This is stagflation, an upward shift in aggregate supply. The most likely cause is increased wage demands due to past inflation. Unemployment was clearly below the NAIRU.
    c. This is a downward shift in aggregate supply.
    d. This is the prime piece of evidence used to argue that the NAIRU increased. Labor force changes may explain this increase.
    e. Apparently aggregate demand decreased in the early period and aggregate supply shifted toward lower prices and higher output later on. This is a normal business cycle recovery pattern. High unemployment during a recession reduces wage increases and eventually a favorable supply shift restores more normal unemployment rates.
    f. In response to fears of reduced oil supplies, oil prices rose and aggregate supply decreased. The decline in consumer confidence and new home sales decreased aggregate demand. The result was higher prices and lower output.

4. *a.* has fallen below, is still above
    b. low; raising rates too high
    c. 2.4; sacrifice

CHAPTER 20   The Quantity Theory and Monetarism

Learning Objectives

1. Describe the Chicago approach and how Milton Friedman's theory is different from the quantity theory.

2. Describe the monetarist transmission process for changes in the money stock.

3. State the Keynesian criticisms of the quantity theory and Friedman's adaptation of the quantity theory.

4. Know the six major issues in the Keynesian-monetarist dispute discussed in this chapter.

*5. State the assumptions and results from Patinkin's real balance approach.

*6. Describe the Brunner-Meltzer model and the implications of empirical results obtained from this model.

Key Terms, Concepts, and Institutions

* Brunner-Meltzer model
  Keynesians
  monetarists
  disequilibrium in the government
    sector
* real balance approach
* outside money
  money illusion

  real effects
* inside money
  quantity theory of money
  transmission process
  Chicago approach
  black box
  credit view
  credit crumble

---

*These items are covered in the appendixes to this chapter.

Self-Test: Completion

1. If the data show little correlation between the deficit and changes in nominal income, the _____ theory is suspect.

*2. Brunner and Meltzer view government bonds and capital as (substitutes/complements).

3. You suffer from _____ if you react to nominal, as opposed to real, variables.

4. Friedman's discussion of the transmission process for monetary policy refers to the _____ rather than the _____ , because he believes that the relevant interest rate is not properly measured by the available data.

5. Money that represents a claim against someone in the private sector is called _____ money.

*6. According to _____ , the economy cannot come to equilibrium unless the budget is balanced.

7. Milton Friedman believes the IS curve is relatively _____ and the LM curve is relatively _____ .

*8. The real balance approach was developed by _____ .

9. For the quantity theory to be valid, causation must run from _____ to _____ , and not vice versa.

10. All three monetarist models spring from the _____ theory.

11. The composition and not just the level of bank and nonbank assets powerfully affect the economy according to _____ .

Self-Test: True-False

1. According to Milton Friedman, the value of k, the proportion of nominal income that people want to hold as money, is a stable number.

2. Keynesians believe that the demand for money is a stable function of variables such as the interest rate and income.

---

*These items are covered in the appendixes to this chapter.

*3. According to Patinkin's real balance approach, monetary variables do not affect real variables in the long run, given completely flexible wages and prices, no money illusion, no redistribution effects, a balanced budget, no government bonds outstanding, and currency as the only type of money.

*4. According to Brunner and Meltzer, if the government issues money to pay for a deficit, prices and nominal income rise permanently.

5. Friedman's version of the quantity theory has been criticized for relying on a black box, that is, relying on the mere correlation of money and income.

*6. A criticism of the Brunner-Meltzer analysis is that it ignores the changes in the stocks of assets.

*7. According to the real balance approach, money is a veil that affects real variables.

*8. In principle, the Brunner-Meltzer approach could produce the Keynesian conclusion that fiscal policy has a powerful effect on income.

*9. Brunner and Meltzer assert that aggregate demand will continue to increase as long as there is a deficit.

*10. If there are government bonds and inside money, the real balance approach asserts that prices and money will not change proportionately.

11. Keynesians believe that income rises less than proportionately to an increase in the money supply.

12. Friedman believes that fiscal policy has a large effect on GDP.

13. If banks were to switch from loans to government securities in an attempt to increase safety, this could cause a recession even though the money supply were unchanged.

Self-Test: Multiple Choice

*1. According to Brunner and Meltzer, an increase in aggregate expenditures will reduce the deficit for all the following reasons *except*
   a. the resulting increase in wealth increases the proportion of income consumed.
   b. the rise in investment and consumption expenditures increases nominal income and, hence, tax receipts.
   c. as nominal income increases, people move into higher tax brackets.

---

*These items are covered in the appendixes to this chapter.

   d. rising prices lower the real value of interest payments on the government's debt.

   e. none of the above; all are reasons why an increase in aggregate expenditures reduces the deficit.

*2. Patinkin assumes all the following *except*

   a. flexible wages and prices.

   b. money and bonds are complements.

   c. people do not suffer from the money illusion.

   d. there are no redistribution effects from changes in prices.

   e. taxpayers are indifferent to the real value of the government's debt.

*3. According to Patinkin's real balance approach, if there are no government bonds outstanding and currency is the only money, a rise in the nominal money stock will increase

   a. the rate of interest.

   b. real income.

   c. prices proportionately.

   d. prices less than proportionately.

   e. the yield on capital.

  4. Which of the following is not a part of Friedman's variant of monetarism?

   a. The IS curve is relatively flat.

   b. The LM curve is relatively steep.

   c. The economy cannot come to equilibrium unless the budget is balanced.

   d. Changes in the money supply go into a black box, and changes in income emerge at the other side.

   e. The quantity theory is the basis for monetarism.

  5. All the following are characteristics of monetarist thought *except* that

   a. the demand for money is a stable function and can be predicted.

   b. the private sector is, for the most part, stable.

   c. prices and wages are relatively stable.

   d. large scale econometric models are more useful than single-equation models.

   e. causation runs from monetary variables to income.

*6. The work of Brunner and Meltzer

   a. takes no account of disequilibrium in the government sector.

   b. develops an explicit transmission mechanism.

   c. concludes that fiscal policy is the dominant impulse that drives nominal income.

*These items are covered in the appendixes to this chapter.

d. stresses the stock of assets and changes in the prices of assets.
e. *b* and *d.*

7. All the following are characteristic of Keynesian thought *except*:
   a. Fiscal policy has powerful effects on the economy.
   b. The long run is the appropriate policy horizon.
   c. An increase in the money supply decreases interest rates, this increases consumption, investment, and net exports, and this in turn increases income.
   d. Prices and wages are sticky.
   e. Stabilization policies are necessary because the private economy is unstable.

*8. According to the Brunner-Meltzer approach, if government spending increases and the government issues money to finance it,
   a. output will temporarily increase.
   b. the price of money in dollar terms falls.
   c. the price of money in dollar terms rises.
   d. the prices of all other items fall.
   e. prices and real income rise permanently.

*9. According to the real balance approach,
   a. creditors experience an increase in real wealth if prices rise.
   b. a uniform change in prices does not affect the value of government debt.
   c. the interest rate depends on real income.
   d. a uniform change in prices does not affect the real value of physical assets.
   e. the demand for labor depends on nominal wages.

*10. The real balance approach specifies that
   a. under certain conditions, changes in the money stock bring about a strictly proportional change in the price level.
   b. people do not suffer from the money illusion.
   c. equilibrium will always occur at full employment if wages and prices are completely flexible.
   d. the existence of government bonds outstanding and inside money implies that money and prices need not change proportionately.
   e. all the above.

11. During the credit crumble of 1990–91
   a. the money supply decreased along with the supply of credit.
   b. banks and S&Ls were usually cautious in the aftermath of the S&L crisis.

*These items are covered in the appendixes to this chapter.

c. capital asset requirements were lowered.

d. banks charged unusually low interest rates.

e. the commercial paper market took advantage of bank difficulties and expanded rapidly.

Topics for Discussion

1. Compare and contrast the three major variants of monetarism.

2. What are the policy implications for each of the three approaches?

*3. Describe the ways in which the Brunner-Meltzer approach differs from the Keynesian approach.

*4. What is Patinkin's major contribution to monetarist thought?

Exercise Questions

*1. According to the Brunner-Meltzer approach,

   a. If the supply of government bonds decreases, the demand for capital (increases/decreases). Investment and income (increase/decrease). Fiscal policy (can/cannot) affect income.

   b. If the government runs a surplus and retires some of its bonds, wealth (increases/decreases), and this causes investment and consumption to (increase/decrease). Aggregate demand (increases/decreases) and income (rises/falls), and this causes tax receipts to (rise/fall). The surplus will (narrow/widen).

2. Put an M next to statements that are consistent with monetarist thinking and a K next to statements consistent with Keynesian thought.

   _____ a. Prices are sticky.
   _____ b. Large-scale econometric models are appropriate for describing how the economy works.
   _____ c. The private sector is inherently stable.
   _____ d. The appropriate policy period is the long run.
   _____ e. The LM curve is inelastic relative to the IS curve.
   _____ f. The demand for money is relatively elastic.
   _____ g. The demand for money is relatively unstable.
   _____ h. In empirical terms, monetary policy and fiscal policy are both effective.
   _____ i. The quantity theory is valid.

---

*These items are covered in the appendixes to this chapter.

_____ *j.* The transmission process for monetary policy is: A decrease in the money supply increases interest rates, this decreases consumption, investment, and net exports, and this in turn decreases income.

Answers to Self-Tests

Completion

1. Keynesian
2. complements
3. money illusion
4. quantity of money, interest rate
5. inside
6. Brunner and Meltzer
7. elastic, inelastic
8. Don Patinkin
9. monetary variables, income
10. quantity
11. the credit view

True-False

1. False
2. False
3. True
4. True
5. True
6. False
7. False
8. True
9. True
10. True
11. True
12. False
13. True

Multiple Choice

1. *e*
2. *b*
3. *c*
4. *c*
5. *d*
6. *e*
7. *b*
8. *a*
9. *d*
10. *e*
11. *b*

Answers to Exercise Questions

1. *a.* decreases; decrease; can
   b. decreases, decrease; decreases, falls, fall; narrow

2. *a.* K
   b. K
   c. M
   d. M
   e. M
   f. K
   g. K
   h. K
   i. M
   j. K

CHAPTER 21

Other Perspectives: New Classical, Real Business Cycle, and Post-Keynesian

Learning Objectives

1. Explain how new classical economists combine rational expectations and market clearing hypotheses to build a competing theoretical framework that leaves little room for demand management.

2. Explain how new Keynesians respond to the new classical challenge by constructing rational microfoundations for Keynesian ideas.

3. Explain how post-Keynesians use uncertainty, financial fragility, and a sociological theory of wages to construct a theory of a rather brittle economy that requires intervention but does not always respond well to traditional tools. This leads post-Keynesians to argue for nontraditional tools.

4. Explain how real business cycle theorists build random technology shocks into a theory of mild cycles and largely voluntary unemployment, leaving demand management unmotivated.

Key Terms, Concepts, and Institutions

new classical
real business cycle
post-Keynesian
microeconomic foundation
implicit contract
hedge finance
new Keynesian

speculative finance
Ponzi finance
flexible prices
rational expectations
sticky wages
Lucas supply function

Self-Test: Completion

1. If someone decides to quit because of a decline in the real wage, then that person is _____ unemployed.

2. According to _____ economists, money demand depends importantly on the state of uncertainty and is therefore not stable.

3. According to post-Keynesians, the _____ side of a bank's balance sheet is relatively more important.

4. If borrowers expect to make their payments from income receipts, then this is _____ finance. If borrowers expect to make payments through additional borrowing, it is _____ finance.

5. If workers attach undue importance to nominal and not real wages, they are said to suffer from _____ .

6. The reluctance of employers to force wage cuts during recessions and workers to demand pay hikes in expansions is referred to as an

    _____ .

7. The idea that wage settlements reflect workers' attitudes, solidarity, and political strength is prevalent among _____ economists.

8. If buyers are able to buy what they want and sellers to sell what they want, then the market is said to have _____ .

9. _____ theorists sometimes argue that most unemployment is frictional.

10. _____ theorists argue that if GDP is above the trend, it is equally likely to move further from the trend as it is to move toward the trend.

11. According to _____ , workers may resist wage cuts in recessions because other workers may not follow and this creates a coordination problem.

Self-Test: True-False

1. According to the new classical model, an anticipated increase in the money supply leads to lower interest rates and higher investment, income, employment, and prices.

2. According to the Lucas supply function, confusion over relative and absolute price changes leads to hedging, which restores a degree of demand-side policy effectiveness.

3. The Great Depression is easily explained by real business cycle theory.

4. Good scientific practice demands that a theory be rejected when the data contradict it.

5. Real business cycle theorists use the fixed costs of employment (commuting, etc.) to explain why people voluntarily quit rather than reduce hours as real wages fall.

6. New classical theorists argue that interest rates should be kept low to reduce income inequality.

7. For many years both Keynesians and monetarists used an error-learning model of inflation expectations.

8. Involuntary unemployment results when workers believe their leisure time is worth more than their wage.

9. Real business cycle theorists use a multiplier-accelerator interaction model to explain business cycles.

10. The critical question facing demand-side and supply-side explanations of business cycles is their relative importance.

11. Firms may resist cutting prices in recessions because it is difficult to predict how rival companies and customers will respond to the move.

12. New Keynesians have provided convincing evidence that identifies which of the many possible reasons for price and wage rigidity is most important.

Self-Test: Multiple Choice

1. According to new classical economics, wages are
   a. sticky.
   b. formed subject to an implicit contract.
   c. flexible because workers know that declining demand will reduce prices so a wage cut won't reduce real wages.
   d. flexible due to the money illusion.
   e. flexible because supply shocks alter productivity.

2. An innovative component of real business cycle theory is that
   a. demand shocks can cause involuntary unemployment.
   b. employment can rise due to a productivity increase leading to higher real wages.
   c. the best prediction of GDP is to assume that the current growth rate will persist regardless of trend growth.
   d. workers form implicit contracts with employers.
   e. money and prices are procyclical.

3. *Animal spirits* refers to
   a. deviations in investment due to gut-level hopes and fears.
   b. the hedging method used in the Lucas supply function.
   c. the random variations in productivity in the real business cycle theory.
   d. the snakelike pattern in the business cycle.
   e. a sneering label used by rational expectationists to describe alternative theories.

4. According to post-Keynesians, restrictive monetary policy
   a. does not alter employment because wages are flexible.
   b. improves the health of banks by increasing interest rates.
   c. can easily lead to bank failures as the present value of loans falls.
   d. will bring inflation down rapidly.
   e. will reduce income inequality.

5. According to Minsky,
   a. Ponzi finance becomes more common in expansions as optimism increases.
   b. bank failures in the past tended to restore hedge finance.
   c. with a great deal of speculative and Ponzi finance, even small drops in income can trigger financial collapse.
   d. if the Fed avoids collapse by lending, it creates inflation.
   e. all the above

6. According to mainstream Keynesians, wages are
   a. flexible because the money illusion is irrational.
   b. sticky because changing wages constantly to reflect differences in productivity is both costly and demoralizing.
   c. sticky because people systematically underestimate changes in inflation rates.
   d. flexible because the cost of unemployment is higher than the cost of renegotiating a wage.
   e. flexible because workers who take a wage cut know other workers will do the same.

7. Many economists object to the Lucas supply function because
   a. much information on changes in aggregate expenditures is available.
   b. it does not use rational expectations.
   c. it assumes the money illusion.
   d. the function predicts longer recessions than actually occur.
   e. it predicts that business cycles are random walks.

8. Critics of real business cycle theory argue that
   a. technology shocks are stronger than real business cycle theorists assume.
   b. money and prices are countercyclical.
   c. real wages are procyclical, counter to the theory.
   d. we ought to see greater variation in the number of hours worked if unemployment is voluntary.
   e. frictional unemployment is highly variable.

9. Uncertainty
   a. can generate unstable investment according to Keynes.
   b. is the key element behind new classical economics.
   c. leads to a stable money demand function.
   d. is easily represented in the IS-LM diagram.
   e. is largely due to government behavior according to Keynes.

10. According to post-Keynesians,
    a. cycles in money cause cycles in income.
    b. cycles in income cause cycles in money through changes in the required reserve ratio.
    c. cycles in income cause cycles in money through changes in the currency-deposit and excess-reserve ratios.
    d. it is legitimate to treat everything else as constant and consider changes in one element at a time.
    e. money demand is unresponsive to interest-rate changes.

11. New Keynesians argue that wages may rationally fail to adjust because
    a. workers expect the money supply will be increased.
    b. workers care more about absolute levels of real wages than wages relative to other workers.
    c. unions protect the interests of nonmembers and members equally.
    d. workers informally agree to work harder in peak periods, help train other employees, etc., in return for job and wage security.
    e. most of the labor force is unionized.

Topics for Discussion

1. Both real business cycle theories and new classical economics stress microeconomic foundations. But once those microeconomic foundations are laid, we still have to learn how individual responses lead to aggregate responses. Do you believe the aggregation problem is likely to be difficult or easy? Keynesian and monetarist models begin with plausible aggregate rules, avoiding the aggregation problem. So one group fails to provide microeconomic foundations, and the other fails to show how the foundations lead to aggregates. Which is better?

2. What are the policy implications of the theories presented? How might advice of a new classicist differ from that of a post-Keynesian if the President ever asked?

3. Since part of the debate is over microeconomic foundations, is introspection a valid method of analysis? That is, do any of these theories remind you of your own behavior, and if not, is that a valid or invalid criticism?

Exercise Questions

1. Take out a coin, any coin. Flip it. If it is heads, make a line on a piece of graph paper that starts at a point A and ends one block to the right and one block up. If it is tails, draw a line from A to a point one block to the right and one block down. Flip the coin again. Continue the line from its end and go right one and up one for heads, right one and down one for tails. Continue until you run out of graph paper.

   a. Does there *appear* to be a cyclical pattern in the graph?

   b. Does the cyclical pattern actually exist?

   c. Which group of economists takes this as supporting evidence?

2. Identify whether each statement is a key element of the real business cycle (R), the post-Keynesian (K), or new classical (C) theory by writing R, K, or C next to it.

   a. Changes in productivity often lead to changes in real wages and employment.

   b. Most unemployment is involuntary.

   c. Productivity changes are largely random.

   d. Uncertainty breeds unstable investment and unstable money demand.

e. Since lower wages lead to lower prices, people must expect prices to fall if wage cuts are to become common.

f. Involuntary unemployment is inherently irrational, since those who would be more than willing to work at the current wage ought to offer to work for slightly less to become employed.

g. When banks make loans, economic activity gets a greater boost than when banks buy securities.

h. Workers and firms are uncertain about how to respond to any given wage or price increase because they are uncertain about the behavior of aggregate wages and prices. This leads to a small response even to aggregate wage and price movements, and so leaves little room for demand management to be effective.

Answers to Self-Tests

Completion

1. voluntarily
2. post-Keynesian
3. asset
4. hedge, Ponzi
5. money illusion
6. implicit contract
7. post-Keynesian
8. cleared
9. Real business cycle
10. Real business cycle
11. new-Keynesians

True-False

1. False
2. True
3. False
4. False—the data may be wrong.
5. True
6. False
7. True
8. False
9. False
10. True
11. True
12. False

Multiple Choice

1. *c*
2. *c*
3. *a*
4. *c*
5. *e*
6. *b*
7. *a*
8. *d*
9. *a*
10. *c*
11. *d*

Answers to Exercise Questions

1. a. The human tendency to see patterns is quite strong, so it is likely that the pattern you plotted will appear cyclical.
    b. No, coin flipping is inherently random. A head one time does not mean a head is any more or less likely the next time.
    c. Real business cycle theorists make a virtue of their inability to explain large cycles by arguing that many cycles are illusory.

2. a. R   e. C
    b. K   f. C
    c. R   g. K
    d. K   h. C

CHAPTER 22   The Goals of Monetary Policy

Learning Objectives

1. Cite the four goals of monetary policy.

2. List the three constraints the Fed faces in trying to achieve its goals.

3. Discuss the conflicts among the Fed's goals.

4. Explain why the Fed is reluctant to reveal which goal is being pursued at the expense of other goals.

5. Explain why the Fed does not coordinate its monetary policy with fiscal policy to eliminate some of the conflicts between its goals.

6. Explain why interest-rate stabilization can force the Fed to monetize the government debt.

7. Argue for and against a single goal for the Fed.

Key Terms, Concepts, and Institutions

high employment
price stability
anticipated inflation
unanticipated inflation
redistribution of income
after-tax return
economic growth
shoe-leather cost

monetizing the debt
interest-rate stability
conflicts among goals
coordination of monetary and
    fiscal policies
government budget
    constraint
constraints on monetary policy

Self-Test: Completion

1. An important conflict between the goals of the Fed is between high employment and _____ stability.

2. The costs of _____ inflation are higher than the costs of _____ inflation.

3. We could achieve both high employment and a low rate of interest by a combination of expansive _____ policy and contractionary _____ policy.

4. The inconvenience of continual trips to get currency as a result of fully anticipated inflation is called _____ .

5. Inflation can result in a negative after-tax interest income because _____ interest is taxed.

6. If the inflation rate is 15 percent, the interest rate is 20 percent, and the tax rate is 50 percent, then the real after-tax return is _____ percent.

7. President Carter voiced the concern that trust in government and social institutions is eroded by _____ .

8. Fluctuating interest rates can redistribute wealth since higher interest rates imply everyone's bond holdings are worth _____ .

9. Both fiscal and monetary policies shift aggregate _____ , and therefore both face the short-run trade-off between _____ and _____ .

10. If Congress passed a law that adjusted all tax brackets and exemptions by 10 percent whenever prices rose 10 percent, then we could say the tax system was _____ for inflation.

Self-Test: True-False

1. There are no costs associated with fully anticipated inflation, since everyone knows about it and takes the proper steps to avoid potential costs.

2. Exchange-rate stability is less important for the United States than it is for countries in which foreign trade accounts for a large percentage of GDP.

3. The optimal level of unemployment is no unemployment.

4. Inflation increases the taxes that corporations pay since depreciation is taxed on a replacement cost basis.

5. When a financial panic threatens, preventing it becomes the primary duty of the Fed.

6. Since inflation increases the value of real property, inflation increases the value of stock prices.

7. Inflation increases the real value of savings.

8. Inflation hurts debtors and helps creditors.

9. Inflation reduces our ability to plan for the future.

10. The Fed could increase investment and growth by reducing inflation and its associated uncertainty.

11. The Fed has treated avoidance of financial panics as its primary function since 1933.

12. The goals of stable exchange rates and stable interest rates are in fundamental conflict.

13. The financial planning of firms is aided by stable interest rates.

14. Interest-rate stability and price stability conflict in the long run.

15. The Fed's freedom of action is constrained by its need to retain the confidence of foreign investors.

Self-Test: Multiple Choice

1. The following is a cost of *anticipated* inflation:
   a. Prices will be out of equilibrium for short periods between price changes.
   b. Taxes are redistributed.
   c. Income is redistributed.
   d. Uncertainty reduces growth.
   e. All the above.

2. All the following are arguments for a single goal for the Fed *except*:
   a. The Fed needs flexibility to do what is required in specific, unforeseeable circumstances.

     b. It would be easier to stabilize the economy if the Fed had the single goal of price stability.

     c. A single goal would force the Fed to pay attention to the long-run effects of its policies.

     d. If the Fed had a single goal, it would be possible to evaluate how well the Fed was doing by seeing how closely it came to its goal.

     e. None of the above; all are arguments for a single goal for the Fed.

3. All the following are reasons why the Fed does not reveal which goal it is pursuing at the expense of other goals *except*:

     a. The proponents of a goal which is not being pursued might join a coalition to trim the Fed's independence.

     b. The Fed's goals are always inconsistent with fiscal policy.

     c. If the Fed does not reveal its goals and is criticized for not achieving a certain goal, the Fed can point to a goal it has achieved, even if the goal is not related to monetary policy.

     d. If the Fed does not reveal its goals, it is difficult for anyone to prove it has not met them.

     e. The Fed's goals may conflict in the short run.

4. In recent years, inflation has

     a. helped the poor.

     b. redistributed income within income classes.

     c. led to high nominal interest rates.

     d. only *b* and *c*.

     e. *a, b,* and *c.*

5. We could stimulate economic growth through a low real interest rate if

     a. the Fed would allow rapid money growth.

     b. both monetary and fiscal policies were tight.

     c. both monetary and fiscal policies were loose.

     d. there was a budget surplus and expansionary monetary policy.

     e. the government reduced its expenditures on research and development.

6. A reduction in interest rates hurts

     a. bondholders.

     b. those who borrow long term and lend short term.

     c. savings and loans.

     d. corporations about to sell bonds.

     e. people with large holdings of commercial paper.

7. The goals of economic growth and price stability

     a. conflict in the long run and in the short run.

  b. conflict in the long run, because price stability increases interest rates.

  c. conflict only in the short run, since price stability may require short-run recessions.

  d. never conflict.

  e. are relatively minor goals.

8. The goals of interest-rate stability and price stability

  a. conflict in both the long and short runs.

  b. conflict in the short run only.

  c. conflict in the long run only.

  d. never conflict.

9. The Fed wants to avoid sharply fluctuating interest rates for all the following reasons *except*:

  a. Financial markets operate more efficiently when interest rates are stable.

  b. Sharply rising interest rates can cause problems for depository institutions with long-term loans to LDCs.

  c. Interest-rate fluctuations induce exchange rate fluctuations.

  d. The public objects to large increases in interest rates.

  e. None of the above; all are reasons the Fed tries to avoid sharply fluctuating interest rates.

10. All the following are results of unanticipated inflation *except*

  a. that borrowers pay too much in taxes because nominal—as opposed to real—interest is taxed.

  b. that stock prices fall.

  c. that retirees on fixed incomes are hurt.

  d. that after-tax profits are less reliable as a guide to the true productivity of capital.

  e. insecurity and uncertainty.

11. The Fed faces a dilemma if it wants to stabilize interest rates in the short run and keep prices stable when interest rates

  a. and prices are rising.

  b. are rising and prices are falling.

  c. and prices are falling.

  d. are falling and prices are rising.

  e. both *a* and *c*.

12. Price stability and high employment come into conflict if

  a. there is deflation and unemployment.

  b. there is inflation and unemployment.

  c. there is inflation and overemployment.

    d.   aggregate demand suddenly drops.

    e.   both *a* and *c.*

Topics for Discussion

1. Should the Fed explain which goal is being pursued at the expense of others?

2. What is the connection between the government's budget constraint and Fed policy?

3. Why can't we use fiscal policy to combat unemployment and monetary policy to combat inflation?

4. If you were in a position to mandate which goal(s) the Fed must pursue, which goal(s) would you choose? Defend your choice.

5. Why is price stability a poor goal if there is a major oil-price increase?

Exercise Questions

Use the IS-LM and aggregate demand–aggregate supply diagrams to illustrate the conflicts in Fed goals.

1. Assume the Fed wishes to maintain the current rate of interest but wants to reduce output in order to reduce inflation. The current economic situation is shown in Figure 22.1.

Figure 22.1   IS-LM Curves

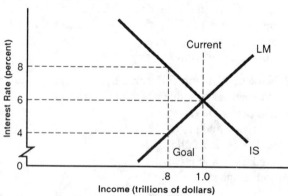

To achieve the income goal the Fed could (*a:* increase/decrease) the money stock. This would shift the (*b:* IS/LM) curve (*c:* up/down). If government policy did not change, the interest rate would be (*d:* 4 percent/6 percent/8 percent). The government could help the Fed to achieve its goals by (*e:* increasing taxes and reducing government spending/reducing taxes and increasing government spending). This would shift the (*f:* IS/LM) curve (*g:* up/down). The two policies (*h:* could/could not) be coordinated to achieve the interest rate and income goals.

Alternatively, if the government (*i:* increased/decreased) government spending to achieve the income goal and the Fed kept the money stock constant, the interest rate would be (*j:* 4 percent/6 percent/8 percent).

2. Assume the Fed wishes to increase employment without changing the price level. The current economic condition is shown in Figure 22.2.

Figure 22.2   Aggregate Supply/Aggregate Demand Curves

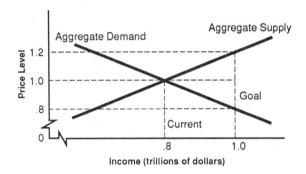

If the Fed acts alone to achieve the income level of $1 trillion, it will (*a:* increase/decrease) the money stock; this will shift the aggregate (*b:* demand/supply) curve (*c:* up/down). The new price level would be (*d:* .8/1.0/1.2). The government (*e:* can/cannot) help, since changes in government spending and taxes affect aggregate (*f:* supply/demand). To resolve this conflict, we need to find some way to (*g:* increase/decrease) aggregate (*h:* supply/demand). Reagan used to claim he had just such a tool in the form of tax cuts. Do you remember the argument?

3. List the four goals of the Fed and the three constraints the Fed takes into account in aiming at these goals.

4.   WASHINGTON—The Federal Reserve, amid strong evidence of a slowing economy, decided to leave short-term interest rates unchanged yesterday.
    . . . The Fed began raising short-term rates in February of 1994 . . . *Wall Street Journal,* May 24, 1995, p. A2.

On the basis of the Fed's actions from February 1994 up to and including May 1995, which goal seemed to be paramount for the Fed during this time period?

Answers to Self-Tests

Completion

1. price
2. unanticipated, anticipated
3. monetary, fiscal
4. shoe-leather cost
5. nominal
6. −5
7. inflation
8. less
9. expenditures, inflation, unemployment
10. indexed

True-False

1. False
2. True
3. False
4. False
5. True
6. False
7. False
8. False
9. True
10. True
11. True
12. False
13. True
14. False
15. True

Multiple Choice

1. a
2. a
3. b
4. e
5. d
6. b
7. c
8. b
9. e
10. a
11. e
12. b

Answers to Exercise Questions

1. a. decrease
   b. LM
   c. up
   d. 8 percent
   e. increasing taxes and reducing government spending
   f. IS

g. down
h. could
i. decreased
j. 4 percent

2.   a. increase
     b. demand
     c. up
     d. 1.2
     e. cannot
     f. demand
     g. increase
     h. supply

3. The four goals of the Fed are: high employment, price stability, an appropriate exchange rate, and a high rate of economic growth. The three constraints are the Fed's need to: prevent financial panics, avoid excessive interest-rate instability, and retain the confidence of foreign investors.

4. The Fed appeared to be favoring price stability as opposed to high employment during this time period.

CHAPTER 23   The Tools of Monetary Policy

Learning Objectives

1. Describe each of the Fed's six tools, how they work, and how the Fed would use them to pursue expansionary and contractionary monetary policies.

3. List the advantages and disadvantages of each of the Fed's tools.

4. Distinguish between dynamic and defensive operations.

Key Terms, Concepts, and Institutions

selective controls	reverse repo (matched sale purchase)
announcement effect	dynamic operations
adjusted credit	defensive operations
extended credit	margin
discounting	moral suasion
repos (repurchase agreements)	open-market operations
"feel of the market"	discount rate

Self-Test: Completion

1. _____ are used when the Fed wishes temporarily to *absorb* reserves.

2. _____ is a process of deducting interest due from the face value of the borrower's promissory note.

3. A repurchase agreement is an example of a _____ operation.

4. _____ credit is short-term credit, intended to tide depository institutions over until they can get other funds.

5. General tools, such as open-market operations, affect the whole economy, while _____ tools affect particular sectors.

6. _____ credit is available when a depository institution experiences special difficulties or when a broad group of depository institutions experiences liquidity strains.

7. The rate the Fed charges borrowing institutions is called the _____ rate.

8. The Fed has the power to set the _____ , or down payment, required when purchasing stock.

9. _____ refers to written or oral appeals from the Fed.

10. An increase in the reserve requirement ratio _____ the money multiplier.

11. Margin requirements have become less effective due to the emergence of _____ markets.

Self-Test: True-False

1. The primary function of required reserves is to provide reserves in the event of an unexpected deposit outflow.

2. The Fed is authorized to deal only in U.S. government Treasury bills in its open-market operations.

3. The Fed uses repos temporarily to provide reserves.

4. Most of the Fed's open-market operations are defensive in nature.

5. Evidence suggests that high margin requirements increase stock-price volatility.

6. An advantage of open-market operations is that they are easily reversed.

7. Borrowing from the discount window increases when the discount rate is low relative to the federal-funds rate.

8. The Fed changes the discount rate frequently, say, once a month.

9. Lowering the discount rate is always a sign of expansionary policy on the part of the Fed.

10. Increases in the discount rate have less political fallout than decreases.

11. After the failure of Drysdale Government Securities, the Fed convinced Chase to cover $160 million of the losses. This is considered an example of effective moral suasion.

Self-Test: Multiple Choice

1. The Fed's most important and frequently used tool is
    a. moral suasion.
    b. open-market operations.
    c. the discount rate.
    d. the reserve-requirement ratio.
    e. changing the margin requirement.

2. All the following are selective tools of the Fed *except*
    a. moral suasion.
    b. Regulation Q.
    c. the discount rate.
    d. the margin requirement.
    e. control over consumer credit during World War II.

3. For its open-market operations the Fed is permitted to buy and sell
    a. banker's acceptances.
    b. state and local government securities.
    c. securities of U.S. government agencies.
    d. Ginnie Mae bonds.
    e. all the above.

4. If the Fed wishes to pursue an anti-inflationary policy, it will probably
    a. sell securities.
    b. buy securities.
    c. lower the discount rate.
    d. lower the reserve requirement ratio.
    e. decrease the margin requirement.

5. If the Fed buys securities in the open market,
    a. the money supply will increase.
    b. the money supply will decrease.
    c. aggregate demand will increase.
    d. aggregate demand will decrease.
    e. *a* and *c.*
    f. *b* and *d.*

6. If the Fed wishes to decrease the overall level of reserves, it will
    a. buy securities.
    b. use one of its selective controls.
    c. use one of its general controls.
    d. sell securities.
    e. *c* and *d.*

7. In January 1995, some analysts believed that concern about rising inflation might cause the Fed to adopt a more restrictive policy. These

analysts expected the Fed to (buy/sell) securities; this would (quicken/slow) the growth of the money supply and push interest rates (up/down) in the short run.

   a.   buy; slow, up
   b.   sell; quicken, up
   c.   sell; slow, up
   d.   sell; quicken, down
   e.   buy; slow, down

8. If the Fed wished to increase the money supply, it would (buy/sell) securities; this would (raise/lower) bond prices.

   a.   buy; raise
   b.   buy; lower
   c.   sell; raise
   d.   sell; lower

9. The reserve requirement ratio

   a.   is the same for ali banks.
   b.   works by affecting the money multiplier.
   c.   is changed frequently.
   d.   is a flexible tool.
   e.   serves to protect depositors.

10. Which of the following tools has no announcement effect?

   a.   Discount rate.
   b.   Margin requirement.
   c.   Moral suasion.
   d.   Open-market operations.
   e.   None of the above; all have announcement effects.

Topics for Discussion

1. What is the difference between defensive and dynamic operations? Which is more visible to the public?

2. What are repos and when are they likely to be used? Give specific examples.

3. Why are changes in the reserve requirement ratio so seldom used?

4. Why does the Fed deal mainly in Treasury bills as opposed to other securities?

5. Explain why the announcement effect of changes in the discount rate can be ambiguous.

6. What is the difference between general and selective tools? Do general tools have an equal impact on all sectors of the economy?

7. Should the Fed allow large-scale failures in financial markets? Can you think of examples in which the Fed has allowed such failures either covered or not covered by the text?

Exercise Questions

1. The August 4, 1983, edition of the *Wall Street Journal* reported that "The Federal Reserve, seeking to offset the expansionary effect of U.S. intervention in foreign-exchange markets, is using its domestic operations to maintain the monetary restraint it began last May," according to Fed Chairman Paul Volcker.

   a. Mr. Volcker is describing (dynamic/defensive) operations.

   b. The Fed probably used (repos/matched sale purchases) to offset its foreign currency intervention.

   c. The federal-funds rate probably (rose/fell) in response to the Fed's domestic market operations.

   d. In response to the Fed's domestic market operations, bond prices probably (rose/fell).

2. Label each of the following actions by the Fed as generally contractionary or generally expansionary.

   a. a rise in the discount rate

   b. a matched sale purchase

   c. an extension of reserve requirements to cover institutions not currently subject to reserve requirements

   d. a decrease in the margin requirement

   e. an increase in the maximum maturity of loans for consumer durables

3. The T account in Table 23.1 represents the balance sheet of the New Haven National Bank. Suppose the Fed buys $1,000 of securities from New Haven. Show how this purchase (increases/decreases) reserves.

Table 23.1 T Account for New Haven National Bank before Fed Purchase

Assets		Liabilities and net worth	
Cash	$1,000	Demand deposits	$5,000
Reserves at the Fed	$2,000	Time deposits	$1,200
Securities	$1,000		
Other gunk	. . . . . .	Other gunk	. . . . . .

In Table 23.2, fill in the T account after the Fed buys securities.

Table 23.2 T Account for New Haven National Bank after Fed Purchase

Assets		Liabilities and net worth	
Cash	$_____	Demand deposits	$_____
Reserves at the Fed	$_____	Time deposits	$_____
Securities	$_____		
Other gunk	. . . . . .	Other gunk	. . . . . .

4. Circle the appropriate responses. If the Fed wished to increase the money supply, it would:

   a. (buy/sell) securities,

   b. (raise/lower) the discount rate,

   c. (raise/lower) the reserve requirement,

   d. raise/lower) the margin requirement, or

   e. (encourage/discourage) banks to increase their lending.

5. . . . Janet Yellen, a Federal Reserve governor, injected a dose of caution into the marketplace when she suggested in a news report that the Fed may not yet have finished its credit tightening . . . *Wall Street Journal,* April 12, 1995, p. C1.

If the Fed continued its credit tightening, its actions would be considered (defensive/dynamic) operations. In response to credit tightening by the Fed, interest rates would (rise/fall) and bond prices would (rise/fall).

Answers to Self-Tests

Completion

1. reverse repos or matched sale purchases
2. Discounting
3. defensive
4. Adjustment
5. selective

6. Extended
7. discount
8. margin

9. Moral suasion
10. decreases
11. futures

True-False

1. False
2. False
3. True
4. True
5. False
6. True

7. True
8. False
9. False
10. False
11. True

Multiple Choice

1. *b*
2. *c*
3. *e*
4. *a*
5. *e*

6. *e*
7. *c*
8. *a*
9. *b*
10. *e*

Answers to Exercise Questions

1. *a.* defensive
   b. matched sale purchases
   c. rose
   d. fell

2. *a.* generally contractionary
   b. generally contractionary
   c. generally contractionary
   d. generally expansionary
   e. generally expansionary

3. increases
   The Fed pays for the securities by increasing New Haven's reserves at the Fed.

Answer to Table 23.2 T Account for New Haven National Bank after Fed Purchase

Assets		Liabilities and net worth	
Cash	$1,000	Demand deposits	$5,000
Reserves at the Fed	$3,000	Time deposits	$1,200
Securities	$ 0		
Other gunk	. . . . . .	Other gunk	. . . . . .

4. *a.* buy   *d.* lower
   b. lower   *e.* encourage
   c. lower

5. dynamic; rise, fall

CHAPTER 24   Targets and Instruments

Learning Objectives

1. Understand the relationships between tools, instruments, targets, and goals.

2. Discuss the Fed's two principal strategies: GDP targeting and intermediate targets and instruments.

3. Explain the advantages and disadvantages of using more than one target.

4. Explain the criteria for target variables, and evaluate the money stock, interest rates, credit or debit variables, and the exchange rate in terms of these criteria.

5. Use the Cambridge equation to explain when the Fed should focus on the money supply and when it should focus on interest rates.

*6. Use the IS-LM model to explain when the Fed should focus on the money supply and when it should focus on the interest rate.

7. Evaluate the Fed's instruments in terms of its criteria.

8. Explain why many economists prefer a nonaccommodating policy and why the Fed has become increasingly accommodative.

9. Discuss briefly the targets and instruments the Fed has used in the decades since the 1950s.

Key Terms, Concepts, and Institutions

You should be able to define or explain

targets	administrative and political feasibility
instruments	base drift

---

*This item is covered in the appendixes to this chapter

unborrowed reserves
measurability
controllability
relatedness
straddle
credit rationing
expected real interest rate
GDP targeting
intermediate targets and
   instruments framework
goals

monetarist experiment
interest-rate target
money-stock target
aggregates
nominal GDP target
real GDP target
accommodating policy
borrowed reserves
information variables
credit as a target

Self-Test: Completion

1. The set of variables closely related to the Fed's goals are called

   _____ .

2. Monetarists prefer the _____ as a target since they believe

   _____ is a stable function of known variables.

3. Perhaps the most serious problem in measuring the interest rate is that
we are not interested in the nominal interest rate but the

   _____ rate of interest.

4. The class of variables between the Fed's tools and its targets are called

   _____ .

5. The fact that *M-1* tends to grow more rapidly in _____ suggests
the Fed is following an accommodative policy.

6. The text speculates that the Fed has been accommodative in an attempt

   to avoid fluctuations in _____ .

7. The Fed usually does not know the money demand function exactly, so it
is difficult to select two consistent money-stock and interest-rate targets.
It therefore picks ranges for each target hoping to

   _____ a consistent point.

8. The shorthand expression for targeting numerous variables that affect

   GDP is _____ .

9. If the IS curve shifts out unexpectedly, then a(n) _____ target is
appropriate.

10. Given a change in the Cambridge k, a(n) _____ target is appropriate.

11. Different reserve and base concepts are referred to collectively as the

    _____ .

12. The wide range of money definitions means that money does not fulfill the _____ criteria for a good target particularly well.

13. If the Cambridge k is stable or a stable function of known variables, then money does fulfill the _____ criteria for a good target.

14. If the Phillips curve is vertical, then the interest rate does not fulfill the _____ criteria for a good target.

15. Ben Friedman has argued that the Fed should include outstanding _____ as one of the variables it watches while deciding on monetary policy.

16. In periods of tight money, rather than fully raise interest rates, banks will sometimes meet the credit needs of their preferred long-term customers by cutting off other less-preferred customers. This is called

    _____ .

17. If the Fed learns that M-2 is growing more slowly than expected, but does nothing, then M-2 is probably a(n) _____ variable.

18. If the Fed is interested in using an accommodating instrument, then instead of total reserves it would use _____ or _____ .

Self-Test: True-False

1. There is no measurement problem if the Fed uses the exchange rate as a target.

2. The use of unattainable targets provides a bureaucracy with an excuse for failure.

3. The Fed can achieve any combination of interest rates and money growth it desires.

4. It is easy to determine the applicable tax rate for the marginal borrower.

5. If the price level is stable, the distinction between the nominal and expected real rates of interest is not a significant problem.

6. Most economists think the short-term interest rate has more effect on investment than the long-term interest rate.

7. We can illustrate the effect of an interest-rate target by drawing a horizontal LM curve.

8. Using a money-stock target allows the crowding-out effect to act as an automatic stabilizer given a shift in the IS curve.

9. If unexpected shifts in the IS and LM curves are equally likely, then the interest rate is a better target than the money stock.

10. Total reserves and unborrowed reserves are accurately measurable.

11. Monetarists believe that total reserves, the least accommodating measure of reserves, is the appropriate instrument for controlling the money stock.

12. If the Fed used a nominal GDP target, there would be no need for a money-stock or interest-rate target.

13. If nominal GDP is kept constant and wage demands lead to higher prices, then output and employment increase.

14. It may be politically easier to announce a money-stock target than an income target if the Fed's income target is considered too low by the public.

15. If the Fed were to hook the discount rate to the federal-funds rate, policy would be less accommodative.

16. Information variables are variables the Fed can control.

17. Interest-rate targets help the Fed keep inflation under control.

Self-Test: Multiple Choice

1. The Fed's use of borrowed reserves as an instrument
   a. increases the Fed's control over money.
   b. allows an increase in money demand to increase money supply.
   c. is universally applauded by economists.
   d. fights inflation because an increase in prices will force up money demand and interest rates.
   e. allows variations in money demand to affect interest rates and income.

2. The Fed should use an interest-rate target when
   a. prices are rising rapidly.
   b. government expenditure is rising rapidly.

    c. investment falls as business executives lose confidence.
    d. *k* changes.
    e. *a, b,* and *c.*

3. Under an interest-rate target, an increase in government spending
    a. still crowds out private investment in the short run.
    b. results in a smaller change in nominal income than under a money-stock target.
    c. results in a larger change in nominal income than under a money-stock target.
    d. leaves nominal income unchanged.
    e. forces the Fed to sell government bonds.

4. Under a money-stock target, an increase in government spending
    a. forces the Fed to buy government bonds.
    b. crowds out private investment in the short run.
    c. leaves nominal income unchanged.
    d. causes nominal income to rise but by less than under an interest-rate target.
    e. both *b* and *d.*

5. An increase in the Cambridge *k*
    a. under a money-stock target leads to lower interest rates and a lower nominal income.
    b. leaves income and interest rates unchanged under an interest-rate target.
    c. under a money-stock target leads to higher interest rates and a higher nominal income.
    d. still reduces income under an interest-rate target but not by as much as under a money-stock target.
    e. could be due to a higher price level.

6. All the following are problems with the measurement of interest rates *except*
    a. credit rationing.
    b. measuring the expected rate of inflation.
    c. constructing an appropriate average.
    d. estimating the impact of taxes.
    e. the vertical Phillips curve.

7. If the long-run Phillips curve is vertical, then any attempt by the Fed to raise output above the natural rate by lowering interest rates will
    a. result in only a temporary reduction in interest rates. The long-run effect will be an increase in the price level.
    b. create a recession.
    c. permanently increase investment, growth, and income.

    d.   increase prices in the short run but not the long run.

    e.   reduce prices and increase income.

8. One of the major criticisms of the Fed over the last few decades is that

    a.   money growth has been procyclical.

    b.   it has given excessive attention to the aggregates.

    c.   it has been unwilling to exercise independent judgment.

    d.   it has refused to help the Treasury finance deficits by buying Treasury bills.

    e.   by openly discussing the reasons for its decisions, it has politicized monetary policy.

9. From a political point of view it might be better to target

    a.   money than interest rates because it may be easier to "sell" a necessary restrictive policy by emphasizing the slow money growth than by pointing to the higher interest rates.

    b.   money than interest rates because focusing on money emphasizes short-term goals.

    c.   interest rates than money because interest rates measure the value of money and the Fed's primary mission is to stabilize money's value.

    d.   real income than nominal income because it is usually more popular to accommodate price increases than fight them.

    e.   both *a* and *d.*

10. Measurement problems include

    a.   the difference between real and nominal interest rates.

    b.   seasonal corrections of the money-supply data.

    c.   whether *M-1*, *M-2*, or some weighted aggregate is the appropriate target.

    d.   before-tax versus after-tax interest rates.

    e.   all the above.

11. Currently, the Fed appears to

    a.   use *M-2* as an information variable, target nominal GDP, and use either unborrowed reserves or the federal-funds rate as an instrument.

    b.   use *M-1* as a target variable and use the base as the instrument.

    c.   use short-term interest rates as the target and federal funds as the instrument.

    d.   have abandoned the instruments, targets, and goals framework.

    e.   be undecided between *a* and *d.*

12. The ratio of long-term to short-term bond yields
    a. decreases as expected inflation rises.
    b. is stable as long as expected inflation is stable.
    c. is directly, although somewhat noisily, related to expected inflation.
    d. is currently used as a Fed instrument.
    e. tends to rise as people become more confident about the future.

13. Free reserves
    a. tend to increase in recessions.
    b. are a good countercyclical instrument.
    c. are total reserves less borrowed reserves.
    d. tend to increase in expansions.
    e. are currently used by the Fed as an instrument.

Topics for Discussion

The June 26, 1992, *Wall Street Journal*, ran an article on page 1 that analyzed policy confrontations with the Fed. Use what you have learned in this chapter to discuss the following paraphrased excerpts.

1. The main issue is whether the economic recovery is continuing on schedule or is about to swoon again as it did in the summer of 1991. Evidence for continued recovery includes: indexes of consumer confidence are up, housing starts are up, and *M-1* growth is high. Evidence of weakness includes: new building permits have declined for three straight months, export growth is slowing, claims for unemployment benefits rose, unemployment remains high, and *M-2* growth was below target for the year and was negative in recent months.

2. Coalitions appear to be forming around a variety of political and economic lines. Bush appointees, Mr. Mullins, Mr. Lindsey, and Ms. Phillips, favor reducing interest rates. The Reagan appointees, Angell, LaWare, and Kelley appear opposed. Two of the five district bank presidents favor *M-1*, which has been growing rapidly. The chairman, Mr. Greenspan, is harder to read but is generally thought to be a staunch inflation foe. Further, Mr. Greenspan argues that the Fed is operating with a "50-mile-an-hour head wind" because business executives and consumers want to reduce their debts, and this makes them less responsive to interest-rate cuts.

3. *M-2* has long been the Fed's measure of choice, but the gauge appears to be broken. Despite a target growth of 2.5 percent, actual growth since January has been 1.8 percent. Some would abandon *M-2*; some want much more data—several years worth of data.

4. The Fed's goals are unclear. Should the Fed be attempting to stimulate the economy, as Bush clearly desires, or should it take this opportunity to finally wring inflation out of the economy?

5. The changes in Fed policy have generally been announced as interest-rate moves. In particular, following the stalled recovery in the summer of 1991 the Fed cut the discount rate a full point. The federal-funds rate is presented in the article as a focal point for internal Fed debate.

6. You have the advantage that much time has passed since this article was written. Was the *M-2* gauge broken? Did the recovery stall out? Did the Fed bow to political pressure? Have consumers and business executives joined the party by spending and going deeper into debt?

Exercise Questions

1. The table below makes use of $M = kPY$ to analyze whether the Fed should use the money supply or the interest rate as a target.

	M (trillions of dollars)	k	Interest rate (%)	P	Y (trillions of dollars)
Base case	$3.5	.5	7	1	$7
Case 1	3.5	.6	8	1	a
Case 2	c	.6	7	1	7
Case 3	3.5	.5	10	1.1	e
Case 4	4.0	.5	7	1.1	f

Case 1. Compared to the base case, case 1 represents an increase in money demand leading to higher rates of interest. In this case the Fed is pursuing a money-stock target and leaves the money supply at $3.5 trillion. The level of real income that preserves $M = kPy$ is (a. _____). In this case, a constant money target leads to (b. a recession/inflation).

Case 2. This time the Fed pursues a constant interest rate target, which leads them to offset the increase in k with a increase in the money supply to (c. _____). Avoiding the interest-rate change allows income to be stable. For the process to occur, the Fed (d. must/need not) know the change in k.

Case 3. Heavy demand causes prices to rise compared to the base case. People demand higher nominal interest rates (why?). Under a constant money-stock rule, income will be (e. _____).

Case 4. If the price increase occurs given an interest-rate target, the Fed increases the money supply and income would be (*f.* _____).

Summing up then, if interest rates and *k* move in the same direction due to a change in money demand, then (*g.* an interest-rate/money-supply) target is best. But, if inflation causes higher interest rates, then

(*h.* _____) target makes the inflation worse by boosting income.

Interest-Rate and Money-Stock Targets Compared. For questions 2 and 3 we have the usual IS-LM curves. The curves intersect at the desired level of output. There is also an LM* curve that represents equilibrium in the money market under an interest-rate target. Such a curve assumes the Fed expands or contracts the money supply to keep the interest rate constant. While the LM* is technically not an LM curve, since such a curve assumes a constant money stock, it is a useful device.

* 2. Assume investors lose confidence and invest less.

    a. Shift the appropriate curve in Figure 24.1 in the correct direction. Compare the new point of intersection of IS and LM, which would be the equilibrium given a money-stock target, with the point on LM*, which would be the new equilibrium given an interest-rate target.

Figure 24.1 IS-LM Curves

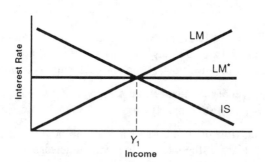

Under the interest-rate target, the change in income is (*b:* larger/smaller) than under a money-stock target. So (*c:* an interest-rate/a money-stock) target is better.

---

*These items are covered int he appendixes to this chapter.

*3. Assume new types of accounts increase money demand.

    a. Shift the appropriate curve in Figure 24.2 in the correct direction. Compare the new point of intersection of IS on LM, which would be the equilibrium given a money-stock target, with the point on LM*, the new equilibrium given an interest-rate target.

Figure 24.2   IS-LM Curves

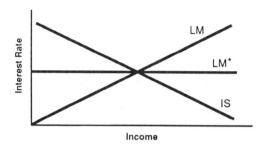

    Under the interest-rate target, the change in income is (*b:* larger/smaller) than under a money-stock target. So (*c:* an interest-rate/a money-stock) target is better.

    Under the interest-rate target, the change in income is (*b:* larger/smaller) than under a money-stock target. So (*c:* an interest-rate/a money-stock) target is better.

Answers to Self-Tests

Completion

1.	targets	11.	aggregates
2.	money stock, *k*	12.	measurability
3.	expected real	13.	relatedness
4.	instruments	14.	controllability
5.	expansions	15.	credit (or debt)
6.	interest rates	16.	credit rationing
7.	straddle	17.	information
8.	GDP targeting	18.	unborrowed reserves,
9.	money-stock		free reserves
10.	interest-rate		

---

*These items are covered in the appendixes to this chapter.

True-False

1.	True	10.	True
2.	True	11.	True
3.	False	12.	False
4.	False	13.	False
5.	True	14.	True
6.	False	15.	True
7.	True	16.	False
8.	True	17.	False
9.	False		

Multiple Choice

1.	*b*	8.	*a*
2.	*d*	9.	*e*
3.	*c*	10.	*e*
4.	*e*	11.	*e*
5.	*b*	12.	*c*
6.	*e*	13.	*a*
7.	*a*		

Answers to Exercise Questions

1.   *a.*   5.8   *e.*   6.4
          b.   a recession   *f.*   7.3
          c.   4.2   *g.*   an interest-rate
          d.   need not   *h.*   an interest-rate

* 2.   *a.*   **Answer to Figure 24.1   IS-LM Curves**

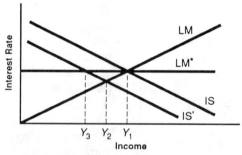

Y_2 = Income Given a Money Stock
Y_3 = Income Given an Interest Rate Target

---

    b.   larger

    c.   money-stock

*3.   *a.*   **Answer to Figure 24.2   IS-LM Curves**

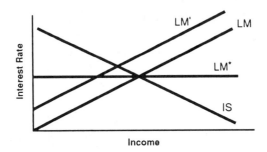

    b.   smaller

    c.   an interest-rate

CHAPTER 25   The Impact of Monetary Policy

Learning Objectives

1. Describe the monetarist transmission mechanism and how it differs from that of income-expenditure theorists.

2. Describe the process by which monetary policy affects consumption and stock prices.

3. Explain how monetary policy affects income through its effects on international trade and credit.

4. Explain the implications of rational expectations theory for monetary policy.

5. Describe the range of econometric estimates of the effects of monetary policy.

Key Terms, Concepts, and Institutions

transmission process
portfolio equilibrium
Income-expenditure transmission
    process
expectations effect
capital rationing effect
stock price effect

consumption channel
investment channel
net exports channel
rational expectations
econometric model
MPS model
credit channel

Self-Test: Completion

1. When the quantity of money increases, the yield on money (increases/decreases).

2. If the Fed pursues a noninflationary expansionary monetary policy, stock prices will (rise/fall).

3. According to the portfolio equilibrium approach, a fall in the money stock will (raise/lower) the prices of all assets in the economy.

4. _____ theorists believe that an increase in the rate of growth of the monetary base could lead to an immediate increase in prices if people expect it to and react accordingly.

5. The _____ the U.S. interest rates are relative to foreign interest rates, the lower net U.S. exports are.

6. As interest rates rise in the United States, the increased purchases of U.S. securities by foreigners work to moderate the rise in the interest rates, which (enhances/reduces) the impact of the Fed's (expansionary/restrictive) policy.

7. The _____ channel focuses on the effect of a restrictive monetary policy on the creditworthiness of potential borrowers.

8. According to the expectations effect, firms respond to monetary expansions by increasing investment because they expect _____ to rise.

9. Capital rationing occurs when banks respond to tight monetary policy, not by raising loan interest rates, but by increasing _____ .

10. The income-expenditure transmission process works largely through effects on

   _____ .

Self-Test: True-False

1. When U.S. interest rates rise, the prices of imported goods also rise.

2. An increase in interest rates is likely to depress stock prices.

3. According to the monetarist transmission process, an increase in the money supply decreases consumption by lowering wealth.

4. A rise in the Aaa-bond rate raises mortgage rates because bonds and mortgages are complements.

5. Foreign claims on U.S. assets are likely to rise when the interest-rate gap (U.S. rate minus foreign rate) rises.

6. If we import more than we export, then foreign claims on U.S. assets must be decreasing.

7. According to the MPS model, the effect of monetary policy on real GDP eventually disappears.

8. If a country buys more claims than it sells to the rest of the world, then it must necessarily import more than it exports.

9. According to rational expectations theorists, if Congress were to order the Fed to make price stability its only goal, the inflation rate would start to decline even before the Fed took any action.

10. If people adjust nominal interest rates for expected inflation due to expansionary monetary policy, then monetary policy is even more effective.

11. According to the portfolio equilibrium model, an increase in the supply of money boosts all asset values, including stocks. As stock prices rise, it becomes cheaper to build new plants than to buy old ones.

12. Given lower interest rates from monetary expansion, wealth and consumption decline.

13. According to the monetarist transmission process, an increase in the money supply causes the imputed yields on consumer durables to exceed other yields, and this increases consumption.

Self-Test: Multiple Choice

1. According to the income-expenditure transmissions process, an increase in the money stock increases *investment* because
   a. stock prices fall.
   b. firms expect their sales to rise.
   c. the present value of a stock's future earnings declines.
   d. of wealth effects.
   e. of liquidity effects.

2. According to the monetarists, decreases in the money stock
   a. decrease investment by decreasing interest rates.
   b. decrease the yield on money.
   c. decrease investment because the value of existing corporations exceeds the cost of creating new ones.
   d. lower the prices of all assets in the economy.
   e. increase the imputed yield on consumer durables.

3. A fall in interest rates
   a. gives households an incentive to hold more consumer durables.
   b. encourages households to buy more securities since their prices will rise in the future.
   c. decreases household liquidity.
   d. encourages households to purchase imported goods.
   e. *a* and *d*.

4. Suppose you have inside information that the Fed intends to pursue a restrictive monetary policy in the next few months. You should
   a. buy stocks.
   b. sell stocks.
   c. buy foreign currency.
   d. sell dollars.
   e. *b* and *c*.

5. A rise in the yield on Treasury securities
   a. increases the Aaa-bond yield.
   b. increases mortgage yields.
   c. decreases housing starts.
   d. decreases investment in industrial plants.
   e. all the above.

6. If U.S. interest rates fall,
   a. the value of the dollar in terms of foreign currencies rises.
   b. the value of the dollar in terms of foreign currencies falls.
   c. U.S. goods cost more in terms of foreign currencies.
   d. imports rise.
   e. *a, c,* and *d*.

7. The international trade effects of expansionary monetary policy in the United States include all the following *except* that
   a. money created in the United States goes, in part, to buy foreign goods and assets.
   b. as we buy more foreign goods and assets, their currencies appreciate and ours depreciates.
   c. the depreciation of the U.S. dollar encourages sales of our goods and reduce sales of foreign goods.
   d. the appreciation of the U.S. dollar tends to increase prices here and reduce prices abroad.
   e. lower interest rates in the United States encourage investors to invest abroad, and this increases the decline in interest rates in the United States.

8. According to 12 models, which statement fairly represents the predicted impact of a 4 percent increase in the money supply in the second year?
   a. There is no area of agreement.
   b. The GDP increases, although the increase may be quite small.
   c. The CPI declines in most, but not all, models.
   d. Those models with a large increase in the CPI also have a large increase in GDP.
   e. The Liverpool model, which relies heavily on rational expectations, gives predictions similar to those of the other models.

9. As a result of restrictive monetary policy,
   a. stock prices are likely to rise.
   b. exports are likely to increase.
   c. imports are likely to decrease.
   d. the value of the dollar will rise against foreign currencies.
   e. small firms will have more access to funds through the credit channel.

10. According to the rational-expectations model, with perfectly flexible prices expansionary monetary policy
    a. has a bigger impact on real GDP than previously believed.
    b. leads to inflation much sooner than other models predict.
    c. reduces nominal interest rates.
    d. affects the exchange rate but not prices.
    e. reduces real GDP.

Topics for Discussion

1. Describe the effects of a restrictive monetary policy according to the monetarist scenario.

2. Why are market imperfections less likely to have an impact on monetary policy in the future?

3. How could an increase in the money supply decrease stock prices?

4. Describe how the effect of monetary policy on international trade reinforces domestic effects.

5. What sectors of the economy (besides residential construction and small businesses) are hurt by restrictive monetary policy?

6. While it may be true that the Fed is not currently held accountable for trade policy, do you think this will continue? Should it continue? Is it rational to blame trading partners for homegrown difficulties? To what extent are the difficulties homegrown?

7. Is the degree of disagreement over the effect of monetary policy major or minor? How would the fact of disagreement affect the policies you would recommend?

Exercise Questions

1. Rep. Stephen L. Neal . . . startled some people recently by introducing a resolution directing the Federal Reserve System "to adopt and pursue monetary policies leading to, and then maintaining, zero inflation." *Wall Street Journal*, November 6, 1989.

   a. What policies would be necessary to achieve this goal?

   b. If the rational-expectations theory is correct, will the goal come at large or small cost?

   c. Would the value of the dollar tend to rise or fall?

   d. How would the exchange rate's behavior alter other countries' plans?

2. The debt binge of the 1980s helped power the bull market of the same period. But now debt is falling fast out of favor . . . .
   If a recession hits the U.S. the earnings and cash flow of many companies will be impaired to a degree that it will be difficult for them to service their debt. *Wall Street Journal*, November 6, 1989.

   a. Does such an effect strengthen or weaken restrictive monetary policy?

   b. Does such an effect have any potential dangers?

3. The dollar bounced back from a one-two punch by central banks, closing higher against the mark and yen.
   Coordinated interest rate increases in Europe and continued dollar selling by central banks, which began on a big scale Sept. 25, would normally decrease the dollar's attraction in global markets. But that happened only briefly yesterday. *Wall Street Journal*, October 6, 1989.

   a. The United States participated in the program to bring the dollar down. Why?

   b. What would the effect of a stronger dollar be on prices here and abroad?

   c. England at this time had a relatively high inflation rate. Would it prefer a stronger or weaker dollar?

   d. The Fed was unwilling to reduce interest rates here to reduce the dollar value; this is why other countries had to increase their rates. Why might the Fed have been reluctant?

4. List the seven channels by which monetary policy affects GDP.

5. Only (*a.* higher/lower) U.S. interest rates can revive the ailing dollar now. . . . But however much the Bundesbank and the Bank of Japan try to bolster the dollar, "it can be defended effectively only from within," says Mr. Persaud [an international economist at J. P. Morgan and Co., in London]. "And that requires monetary policy changes in the United States." *Wall Street Journal,* April 4, 1995, p. C1.

   b. What type of change in U.S. monetary policy is required to strengthen the dollar?

   c. Did the Bundesbank and the Bank of Japan buy or sell dollars in their efforts to bolster the U.S. dollar? Why would they do this?

Answers to Self-Tests

Completion

1.	decreases	6.	reduces, restrictive
2.	rise	7.	credit
3.	lower	8.	sales
4.	Rational-expectations	9.	credit requirements
5.	higher	10.	interest rates

True-False

1.	False	8.	False
2.	True	9.	True
3.	False	10.	False
4.	False	11.	True
5.	True	12.	False
6.	False	13.	True
7.	True		

Multiple Choice

1.	*b*	6.	*b*
2.	*d*	7.	*d*
3.	*a*	8.	*b*
4.	*b*	9.	*d*
5.	*e*	10.	*b*

Answers to Exercise Questions

1. *a.* Restrictive monetary policy.
    b. The cost should be small as people take wage and price cuts, rather than lose sales or experience unemployment.
    c. A restrictive monetary policy would increase the dollar value by increasing interest rates and reducing inflation. Both would increase the attractiveness of our goods and assets to foreigners.
    d. Low U.S. inflation would tend to draw sales from countries with higher inflation. Countries would be forced either to follow the U.S. lead or allow their currency to depreciate.

2. *a.* Strengthen. As a restrictive policy creates a recession, stock values of highly indebted corporations decline; this reduces wealth, consumption, and investment in new enterprises.
    b. The danger was pointed out by Hyman Minsky. If corporations can't meet debt payments due to a recession, waves of nonpayment can sweep through an economy as each corporation was counting on the other to pay, so they could meet their debt obligations. Minsky even argues that the effect—an atom bomb effect—can make policy so strong that it is too dangerous to use.

3. *a.* The United States fretted over a large and persistent trade deficit that a higher dollar would only worsen.
    b. A stronger dollar makes foreign goods cheaper to us, and this reduces inflation here. But since our goods seem more expensive abroad, inflation would rise there.
    c. The English wanted a weak dollar so U.S. goods would be cheap.
    d. The Fed was worried about inflation. It wanted to see clear signs of a weak economy before it would allow interest rates to fall.

4. The seven channels are: investment, expectations, capital rationing, stock prices, consumption, net exports, and credit.

5. *a.* higther
    b. A restrictive monetary policy is necessary to strengthen the dollar.
    c. The Bundesbank and the Bank of Japan bought dollars. A weak dollar makes German and Japanese goods expensive for U.S. customers.

CHAPTER 26   Can Countercyclical Monetary Policy Succeed?

Learning Objectives

1. Explain how countercyclical monetary policy can increase the variance of the income path even if the effects of policy on income and the naturally occurring deviations in income are not correlated.

2. Recognize the difficulties that lags in the effect of policy produce.

3. Explain the implications of the rational-expectations hypothesis for monetary policy.

4. Explore some of the political and administrative problems that inhibit stabilization policy.

Key Terms, Concepts, and Institutions

countercyclical policy
variance
correlation
distributed lag
inside lag
Lucas critique
political business cycles

public-interest theory
public-choice theory
time inconsistency
new classical economists
outside lag
rational expectations

Self-Test: Completion

1. The square of the standard deviation of a variable about its trend is known as the _____ .

2. The impact of monetary policy on nominal income is felt gradually over time. This is called the _____ of policy.

3. While estimates of the impact of monetary policy vary considerably, most agree it takes at least _____ quarters for policy to achieve half its ultimate effect.

4. The time between recognition of the need for corrective action and the Fed's corrective action is called the _____ lag.

5. The time between taking the corrective action and its impact is called the _____ lag.

6. Instead of looking at the policy tool's strength, one should use that tool with the most _____ impact.

7. The Fed may find it useful to avoid clearly stating _____ so that it can convince various interest groups that their interests are given sufficient importance.

8. One of the Keynesian justifications for countercyclical policy is that wages are _____ .

9. The rational-expectations approach blames unemployment on

   _____ .

10. _____ theory argues that government agencies try to maximize their own welfare.

11. Some rational-expectations theorists have argued that only a(n)

    _____ increase in monetary growth will increase nominal income even temporarily.

12. Committees that ignore evidence and reassure themselves all is well have fallen victim to _____ .

Self-Test: True-False

1. According to public-choice theory, the Fed is guided in its actions by what is best for the country.

2. The Lucas critique argues that the existence of rational expectations makes econometric models useless for predicting the impact of macroeconomic policies.

3. The inside lag can be negative.

4. Since the effects of policy occur over time, if the Fed wants to achieve any particular goal rapidly, it will find itself taking measures to counteract its past policy once the goal is reached.

5. There is some limited evidence that suggests the outside lag of monetary policy is highly variable.

6. Stronger tools, even if their impact is somewhat less predictable, are better tools.

7. According to rational-expectations theory, new policies based on an examination of past behavior have a weak foundation given that people may change their behaviors in response to the new policy.

8. If people come to expect tax reductions in recessions and tax increases in inflations, then the change in consumption due to the tax changes will be larger.

9. One possible explanation of the fact that prices are now rising in recessions is that people expect countercyclical policy during a recession.

10. Rational-expectations theory explains periods of unemployment by saying it takes time for employers and workers to recognize that the demand shifts they see in their own industries are both long lasting and the result of an aggregate-expenditures shift and not just a change in relative demand.

11. According to rational-expectations theory, people will react no differently to announced changes in aggregate expenditures than to unannounced changes.

12. Since rational-expectations theory implies that policy can have no systematic effect, stabilization policy leaves the variance of nominal income no larger and no smaller than it would be in the absence of stabilization policy.

13. According to the text, monetary policy will exert a stabilizing influence even if the Fed's timing is right only half the time.

14. One way to explain the rational-expectations hypothesis is to notice that people are not rocks. While you may be able repeatedly to hit a rock

with a hammer, the only way you will be able to hit a person is if it is unexpected.

15. A car with a distributed lag steering mechanism would be easy to control.

16. Time inconsistency refers to the idea that the Fed may want to fool people into working more; this leads to complicated dynamics as people learn to distrust the Fed.

Self-Test: Multiple Choice

1. Assume it takes the Fed about one-quarter of recessionary experience to initiate countercyclical policy. Given the average postwar recession

    of _____ months and the fact it takes at least _____ quarters for half of the impact of policy to be felt, we can say most of

    the impact of policy will be felt _____ the recession.
    a. 20, 8, after
    b. 30, 4, during
    c. 10, 2, after
    d. 5, 1, during
    e. 45, 20, after

2. Stabilization policy is likely to be more successful if
    a. monetary policy has a strong effect on income.
    b. the outside lag is long.
    c. expectations are rational.
    d. we can predict nominal income accurately.
    e. the Fed delays action until a strong consensus forms.

3. The inside lag would be shorter if
    a. the Fed began to take action to offset predicted deviations in income.
    b. investment responded more quickly to changes in the rate of interest.
    c. long-term interest rates responded more quickly to changes in the short-term rate of interest.
    d. prices were more flexible.
    e. all the above.

4. New classical economists
    a. accept the rational-expectations approach.
    b. reject the notion that wages and prices are flexible.

    c.   consider monetary policy more effective than fiscal policy for stabilization purposes.

    d.   assert that a painful recession is not necessary to curb inflation.

    e.   oth *a* and *d*.

5. According to the rational-expectations argument, unemployment is caused by
   - *a.* the difference between planned and actual investment.
   - *b.* the low level of planned investment.
   - *c.* inflexible prices.
   - *d.* the fact that different inputs become fully employed at different levels of income.
   - *e.* the fact that it takes time for unemployment and a general lack of demand to be considered persistent.

6. All the following are necessary for political business cycles to occur *except* that
   - *a.* the Fed must be willing to do the President's bidding.
   - *b.* voters must be aware of the Fed's action in adopting an expansionary policy before an election.
   - *c.* the Fed must be able to time the impact of its policies well.
   - *d.* voters must be influenced by recent economic conditions.
   - *e.* none of the above; all are necessary for political business cycles to occur.

7. Public-interest theory suggests that the
   - *a.* Fed will try to avoid conflict with powerful people.
   - *b.* Fed will be unwilling to give up any of its tools.
   - *c.* Fed will be unwilling to admit past mistakes.
   - *d.* Fed's errors are due to the complexity of its problems.
   - *e.* Fed will act myopically.

8. Not all the implications of rational expectations are negative. Announcement effects could help
   - *a.* by increasing the impact of a tax cut that is described as temporary.
   - *b.* because an expected increase in the money supply has a more predictable effect than an unexpected increase.
   - *c.* because an announced anti-inflation policy may need less unemployment to reduce inflation.
   - *d.* because an announced increase in government spending is more likely to raise real income than prices.
   - *e.* because if everyone knows the money stock will be increased in a recession, recessions will not occur.

9. Robert Hetzel argues that Congress could reduce the Fed's independence if the Fed pursued distasteful policies. To avoid this, the Fed
   a. demands that the Congress state explicit goals for the Fed to follow.
   b. clearly states its goals to avoid confusion.
   c. avoids clearly stated policies, goals, or methods of analysis in order to avoid conflict.
   d. emphasizes future GDP over current GDP.
   e. moves quickly and decisively on the basis of preliminary data.

10. If the distributed lag of the effect of monetary policy is long and variable, then
   a. the correlation coefficient between policy and the natural income path cannot be negative.
   b. expectations are not rational.
   c. policy taken to end a bust could end up accentuating a boom.
   d. countercyclical policy is always harmful.
   e. countercyclical policy is always beneficial.

Topics for Discussion

While Chapter 26 argues that Keynes's ambition to use monetary policy to stabilize the economy on a continuous basis was a vain hope, there is more to his writing. In this regard, the following quotes from The Collected Writings of John Maynard Keynes *are worth considering.*

1. Many of the greatest economic evils of our time are the fruits of risk, uncertainty, and ignorance. It is because particular individuals, fortunate in situation or in abilities, are able to take advantage of uncertainty and ignorance, and also because for the same reason big business is often a lottery, that great inequalities of wealth come about; and these same factors are also the cause of the unemployment of labour, or the disappointment of reasonable business expectations, and of the impairment of efficiency and production. Yet the cure lies outside the operations of individuals; it may even be to the interest of individuals to aggravate the disease. I believe that the cure for these things is partly to be sought in the deliberate control of the currency and of credit by a central institution, and partly in the collection and dissemination on a great scale of data relating to the business situation, including the full publicity, by law if necessary, of all business facts which it is useful to know.[1]

2. Furthermore, it seems unlikely that the influence of banking policy on the rate of interest will be sufficient by itself to determine an optimum rate of

[1] John Maynard Keynes, *The Collected Writings of John Maynard Keynes,* 30 vols. (New York: St. Martins Press for the Royal Economic Society, 1972), vol. 9, p. 292.

investment. I conceive, therefore, that a somewhat comprehensive socialization of investment will prove the only means of securing an approximation to full employment; though this need not exclude all manner of compromises and of devices by which public authority will cooperate with private initiative. But beyond this no obvious case is made out for a system of State Socialism which would embrace most of the economic life of the community. It is not the ownership of the instruments of production which it is important for the State to assume. If the State is able to determine the aggregate amount of resources devoted to augmenting the instruments and the basic rate of reward to those who own them, it will have accomplished all that is necessary.[2]

3. The full employment policy by means of investment is only one particular application of an intellectual theorem. You can produce the result just as well by consuming more or working less. Personally I regard the investment policy as first aid. In U.S. it almost certainly will not do the trick. Less work is the ultimate solution (a 35-hour week would do the trick now).[3]

4. Moderate planning will be safe if those carrying it out are rightly oriented in their own minds and hearts to the moral issue. . . . But the curse is that there is also an important section who could almost be said to want planning not in order to enjoy its fruits but because morally they hold ideas exactly the opposite of yours, and wish to serve not God but the devil.[4]

5. The time may arrive a little later when the community as a whole must pay attention to the innate quality as well as to the mere numbers of its future members.[5]

Exercise Questions

1. The error-learning model used to be a popular way of describing expectations formulation until the rational-expectations theorists showed that it led to systematic errors. As you work through this exercise you'll see why.

    Assume some variable has been rising at a 5 percent rate for the last few months and slows to a 4 percent rate. The error-learning model will project next month's growth rate to be (*a:* greater than/less than/equal to) 4 percent. The growth rates for the following months turn out to be 2 percent, then 1 percent, and then –1 percent. Someone using an error-

[2] Ibid., vol. 7, p. 378.
[3] Ibid., vol. 27, p. 384.
[4] Ibid., vol. 27, p. 387.
[5] Ibid., vol. 9, p. 292.

learning model will consistently predict growth rates that are (*b:* higher than/lower than/equal to) the actual rate. Someone with rational expectations (*c:* will/will not) guess at the turning points between growth and decline and (*d:* will/will not) use the experience of past cycles to make guesses that (*e:* are more precise/while they may be just as imprecise, avoid systematic error).

2. In order to illustrate the variance formula, let income be $4 billion above the desired trend one year, $4 billion below trend the next year, $4 billion above trend the third year, and, finally, $4 billion below trend the fourth year. Policy adds $1 billion to income the first two years and subtracts $1 billion from income the final two years. If we let x represent the deviations from trend of the natural income path, y represent the impact of policy on the deviations of income, and z represent their sum, we have

    $x = +4 -4 +4 -4$
    $y = +1 +1 -1 -1$
    $z = +5 -3 +3 -5.$

    a. Add the absolute values of all the numbers in the series x and divide by 4. This is the average absolute deviation.

    b. Using the same technique, find the average absolute deviation of z.

    c. If the goal of policy is to minimize the average absolute deviation of income, has policy been harmful?

    d. Calculate the variances of the series x, y, and z. This can be done by summing the squares of the entries in each series and dividing the total by 4.

    e. If the goal of policy is to minimize the variance of income, has policy been harmful?

    f. Notice that the variance of z equals the sum of the variances of x and y. What does this imply about the correlation of x and y? (Hint: Use the formula presented on page 457 of the text.)

    g. Explain why your answer in *f* makes sense.

3. A marvelous short story by James Thurber, "The Little Girl and the Wolf," illustrates the concepts of rational expectations and policy ineffectiveness. The story updates Little Red Riding Hood. In Thurber's more modern version Red immediately recognizes the wolf for what he is, pulls a gun from her goody bag, and shoots the wolf dead. Thurber

closes with the moral: "It is not so easy to fool good little girls nowadays as it used to be."[6]

Your task is to explain how the fable illustrates rational-expectations theory.

Answers to Self-Tests

Completion

1.	variance	7.	goals
2.	distributed lag	8.	sticky
3.	two	9.	forecast errors
4.	inside	10.	public choice
5.	outside	11.	unexpected
6.	predictable	12.	group think

True-False

1.	False	9.	True
2.	True	10.	True
3.	True	11.	False
4.	True	12.	False
5.	True	13.	False
6.	False	14.	True
7.	True	15.	False
8.	False	16.	True

Multiple Choice

1.	c	6.	b
2.	d	7.	d
3.	a	8.	c
4.	e	9.	c
5.	e	10.	c

Answers to Exercise Questions

1.   a.   greater than
        b.   higher than
        c.   will

---

[6]James Thurber, *Fables for Our Time* (New York: Harper & Row, 1939), p. 5.

    d. will

    e. while they may be just as imprecise, avoid systematic error

2.   *a.* 4.

    b. 4.

    c. No.

    d. The variance of x is 16.

        The variance of y is 1.

        The variance of z is 17.

    e. Yes.

    f. The coefficient of correlation between x and y is zero, otherwise the variance of z would not be the simple sum of the variances of x and y.

    g. This makes sense because positive or negative values of x are as likely to be associated with positive values of y as with negative values. Knowing the value of a particular x tells us nothing about the value of the corresponding y.

3.   Little Red Riding Hood is assumed to be rational enough to distinguish a wolf from a grandmother and to forecast the behavior of the wolf. Given this, she takes appropriate countermeasures and renders the wolf's policy ineffective. Similarly, if the Fed attempted to reduce real wages through inflation, and thereby stimulate employment, rational-expectations theorists suggest workers would take countermeasures in the form of higher wage demands and render the Fed's policy ineffective. Workers have the more difficult task of determining whether the Fed's policy is wolfish or grandmotherly and may make mistakes, but these mistakes should not be systematic. The moral reminds us that behavior changes with experience—just as rational-expectations theorists insist.

CHAPTER 27   The Record of Monetary Policy

Learning Objectives

1. Cite the four guiding ideas for the Fed when it was established in 1913.

2. Outline the salient points about monetary policy during the Great Depression according to Milton Friedman and Anna Schwartz, and explain the counterarguments by Peter Temin.

3. Explain how credit, debt, and liquidity factors contributed to the length and severity of the Great Depression.

4. Outline the critical episodes in monetary history since the Fed's inception in 1913.

5. Evaluate critically the Fed's performance during each of the critical episodes in monetary history.

Key Terms, Concepts, and Institutions

real-bills doctrine
eligible paper
pegged interest rates
the Accord

credit crumble
the Great Inflation
"Saturday night special"

Self-Test: Completion

1. According to _____ , deposit creation cannot be inflationary if deposits are created as a result of short-term self-liquidating loans that finance real activities.

2. _____ was the term used for promissory notes banks had discounted for their customers that met the requirements of the real-bills doctrine.

3. According to Milton Friedman and Anna Schwartz, the Fed pursued a
   _____ policy during the Great Depression.

4. During the Great Depression, the velocity of money _____ .

5. According to Peter Temin, the decline in _____ caused the
   decline in _____ .

6. The Fed's policy during World War II was to _____ interest
   rates.

7. The agreement reached by the Fed and the Treasury in 1951 was called

   _____ .

8. There is considerable agreement that _____ was the initiating
   factor for the Great Depression.

9. According to the text, the leading candidate to explain the *severity* of
   the Great Depression is _____ .

10. The Fed announced its intention to pay more attention to monetary
    aggregates and less attention to interest rates in _____
    (month and year).

Self-Test: True-False

1. Adherents of the credit view of the Great Depression, such as Ben
   Barnanke and Charles Colormiri, stress the liabilities sides of the banks'
   balance sheets, as opposed to the decreases in banks' assets.

2. According to the credit view, the Great Depression lasted so long in part
   because borrowing relationships were disrupted by bank failures and
   new borrowing relationships had to be established.

3. The decline in the monetary stock during the Great Depression was due
   to a decline in the monetary base.

4. For the decade 1929 to 1939, real interest rates exceeded nominal
   interest rates.

5. Keynesians attribute the decline in the velocity of money that occurred
   during the Great Depression to low interest rates.

6. Temin argues that the stock of money declined during the Great
   Depression because income fell and reduced the demand for money.

7. During World War II the main goal of the Fed was to keep interest rates low to accommodate the Treasury's financing needs.

8. The Fed was in effective control of the money stock during World War II.

9. The 1991 credit crumble was due partly to increased conservatism on the part of banks in light of the preceding rise in bank failures.

10. The inflation of the 1960s was primarily due to supply shocks.

Self-Test: Multiple Choice

1. When the Fed was inaugurated in 1913, its *major* goal was
   a. maintenance of the gold standard.
   b. avoiding financial panics.
   c. stabilizing interest rates.
   d. controlling inflation.
   e. all the above.

2. The decline in the money stock during the Great Depression was due to
   a. a decline in the monetary base.
   b. banks choosing to hold more reserves to deposits.
   c. the public choosing to hold more currency to deposits.
   d. all the above.
   e. only b and c.

3. According to Friedman and Schwartz, the decline in the money stock during the Great Depression was the result of
   a. a shift in the demand for money.
   b. a decrease in income.
   c. an exogenous drop in consumption.
   d. a leftward shift in the supply curve of money.
   e. all the above except d.

4. Temin argues that interest rates were low during the Depression because
   a. the demand for liquid securities increased due to the public's unwillingness to hold illiquid assets.
   b. the demand for money decreased.
   c. the money stock increased.
   d. the inflation rate declined.
   e. none of the above.

5. The great debate between the Fed and the Treasury after World War II
   a. resulted in the 1951 agreement known as the Accord.
   b. was over the control of the money stock.
   c. pitted the Treasury's desire for low interest rates against the Fed's desire for a tighter policy to combat inflation.
   d. resulted in higher short-term interest rates.
   e. all the above.

6. The recovery that started in November of 1982 is unusual because
   a. the federal deficit was low.
   b. there was a large import deficit.
   c. inflation had risen.
   d. inflation had not risen.
   e. the unemployment rate was extremely low.

7. The Fed currently targets
   a. *M-1*.
   b. *M-2*.
   c. *M-3*.
   d. all the above.
   e. *b* and *c*.

8. The Great Inflation was caused by overly expansionary monetary policy. The expansionary monetary policy was in turn caused by
   a. overestimates of the NAIRU by the FOMC.
   b. targeting money rather than interest rates.
   c. political pressure on the Fed.
   d. the need to defend a rapidly falling dollar.
   e. fear that contractionary policy would induce a bank panic.

9. The bond market collapsed in 1980
   a. as a result of the collapse of the mortgage market.
   b. because investors feared that interest rates would fall as a result of unprecedented growth in the money stock.
   c. because investors feared that inflation, and therefore also interest rates, would skyrocket.
   d. because the marginal efficiency of investment shifted inward.
   e. due to an unexplained shift in consumption.

10. All the following were part of President Carter's March 1980 program to break inflationary expectations *except*
   a. raising the reserve requirement on certain managed liabilities.
   b. imposing a reserve requirement on increases in the assets of money-market funds.

    c. imposing a reserve requirement on unsecured consumer loans.
    d. instituting mandatory wage and price controls.
    e. placing a surcharge on the discount rate paid by large banks that borrowed frequently.

11. The credit crumble
    a. occurred in 1933 just before the bank holiday.
    b. was due to new capital requirements and increased caution on the part of banks and examiners.
    c. implied that lower interest rates would increase investment more than usual.
    d. was caused by expectations of inflation reducing bank confidence.
    e. was nothing more than the normal reduction in loan activity during a recession.

Topics for Discussion

1. Why was it odd for a Democratic President to request that the Fed follow a restrictive monetary policy, as President Carter did in 1978?

2. Discuss in detail how recent financial innovations have clouded the interpretation of *M-1* and why the Fed has temporarily decided to let *M-1* rise above its target.

3. What is the problem with wage and price controls as an antidote to inflation?

Exercise Questions

1. The *Wall Street Journal* reported on September 13, 1983, another attempt by the Fed to lean against the wind: "Worries about the federal government's huge end-of-the-quarter borrowing operation helped depress bond prices yesterday, erasing some of the large gains registered recently.

    "The bond markets had rallied strongly in the last few weeks because of a sharp slowing in the growth rate of the nation's money supply. With the money measure well within the Federal Reserve System's target range, many analysts contend the central bank may soon be able to ease credit conditions, paving the way for lower interest rates. . . .

    "The Fed began to tighten its credit clamp last May in an effort to keep the economic recovery from becoming overheated. Some analysts say the maneuver worked."

    a. Before the 1951 Federal Reserve–Treasury Accord, what would you have expected the Fed to do in response to the Treasury's borrowing operations?

    b. If the *Journal* had been reporting a similar story before the October 1979 policy initiative, what measure would the analysts have been watching, as opposed to the money supply?

2.   The *Wall Street Journal* reported on October 6, 1986 (p. 1), that "Paul Volcker, who usually speaks last in Federal Reserve policy debates, surprised his colleagues at an important meeting July 8. The Fed chairman spoke first, and he made it clear that he wanted to lower interest rates.

    "Mr. Volcker's comments were particularly striking because just five months earlier, at a February 24 meeting, he had strenuously resisted an interest rate cut. Indeed, he had nearly quit when four Reserve Board members appointed by President Reagan outvoted him, his first such defeat since becoming chairman in 1979."

    The article goes on to say that the year 1986 marked a turning point in the Volcker era. Given the Fed's monetary policy under Volcker, what was the new emphasis?

3.   In November 1989 the issues facing the Fed were prolonging the longest expansion on record versus fighting inflation. So many recent recessions have begun as deliberate policy to control inflation that "a notion— unfortunately mistaken—has taken hold that if only inflationary pressures can be held in check, the economy will move indefinitely along an expansionary path." Alfred Malabre, *Wall Street Journal*, October 2, 1989.

    Two camps have developed: one camp pleads for lower interest rates and the other to keep interest rates high. How might each camp justify its position?

4.   Despite expectations of weak economic data during the first week in June, 1995, the Federal Reserve did not ease its monetary policy. "Some economists believe that the weak dollar's effect on U.S. inflation may keep the Fed from cutting interest rates soon." *Wall Street Journal*, May 30, 1995, p. A1.

    a. What is the weak dollar's effect on inflation?

    b. What does this article suggest was the Fed's major concern at this time?

Answers to Self-Tests

Completion

1.	the real-bills doctrine	6.	peg
2.	Eligible paper	7.	the Accord
3.	tight	8.	monetary tightness
4.	fell	9.	debt deflation
5.	income, money stock	10.	October 1979

True-False

1.	False	6.	True
2.	True	7.	True
3.	False	8.	False
4.	True	9.	True
5.	True	10.	False

Multiple Choice

1.	*a*	7.	*b*
2.	*e*	8.	*c*
3.	*d*	9.	*c*
4.	*b*	10.	*d*
5.	*e*	11.	*b*
6.	*d*		

Answers to Exercise Questions

1. *a.* The Fed would have increased the money supply by buying the Treasury's securities at a low rate of interest.

   b. Probably they could have been watching the federal-funds rate and other short-term rates.

2. Speculation about Volcker's turnaround takes up at least three different themes: One article argued that it represented a shift from an emphasis on inflation fighting to an emphasis on economic stimulation. Reagan's appointees were genuinely concerned that a recession might develop in 1986. The second emphasizes exchange rates; proponents of this believed Volcker was worried that an interest reduction would reduce the dollar's value even further, and it was already falling dramatically. So Volcker's turnaround would have allowed him the extra time necessary to contact the central banks of Germany and Japan and arrange coordinated interest rate reductions. The third contended that

the change was part of an internal power struggle in which Volcker and Martin were vying for control.

3.   Higher interest rates reduce economic activity and act as a drag on wages and prices. If inflation control is all that is needed to avoid a recession, this may work. However, if business confidence is already declining so that the IS curve has shifted toward lower income, a reduction in output and employment can only be avoided by shifting the LM curve toward higher income and lower interest rates.

4.   *a.*   A weak dollar makes imports more expensive and heightens inflation.

     b.   The Fed was concerned that the economy had reached capacity and that further expansion would only generate inflation. Therefore it wanted to keep interest rates high to bolster the dollar and control inflation.

CHAPTER 28   Alternative Monetary Standards

Learning Objectives

1. Evaluate alternative monetary standards such as feedback rules, the gold standard, private money, currency boards and a populist standard.

2. Explain why the Fed supports limits on its own power.

3. Explain why most economists continue to support considerable discretionary powers for the Fed.

Key Terms, Concepts, and Institutions

monetary standard   feedback rules
currency board   populist standard
private money   gold standard

Self-Test: Completion

1. The system of rules, traditions, and attitudes that govern the money supply is called the _____ .

2. The case for a money growth rate rule was severely undermined in the early 1980s when velocity, which had been _____ , began to _____ .

3. A rule that sets the money growth rate according to an equation containing current and past income growth is known as a _____ .

4. The populist standard maintains that inflation should be controlled by a(n) _____ policy rather than monetary policy.

5. The _____ can be thought of as a rule that forces the central bank to set the price of domestic currency equal to the price of gold.

6. The _____ can be thought of as a rule that forces the central bank to set the price of domestic currency equal to a bundle of foreign currencies.

7. Private money might allow a single private issuer of money to become a monopolist due to _____ .

8. A gold standard could imply high inflation if the supply of gold _____ .

9. If there were pressure for the dollar to decline in value, then, under a gold standard, the Fed would have to _____ the money supply.

10. If velocity is unstable, but money stable, then _____ is unstable.

Self-Test: True-False

1. Monetarists want to increase the scope of the Fed's discretion so that it may more aggressively pursue countercyclical policy.

2. Monetarism lost support as the Fed demonstrated it had the political courage to reduce inflation.

3. Feedback rules make no allowance for variations in velocity.

4. The core idea behind private money is to allow competition so that if the central bank provided a medium of exchange that was a poor store of value, people could switch to a private issuer.

5. High inflation in a country with a currency board will reduce exports.

6. High inflation in a country with a gold standard will increase exports.

7. Congress attempted to force a low inflation goal on the Fed, but the Fed refused.

8. Evaluating feedback rules is difficult because people may change their behaviors if they know the Fed is using such a rule.

9. One of the arguments for a feedback rule is that our ability to predict changes in velocity has become so good that we need to force the Fed to accommodate changes.

10. Hard-line monetarists believe in an independent central bank that is allowed a great deal of discretion.

246 / CHAPTER 28

Self-Test: Multiple Choice

1. The difference between Bennet McCallum's feedback rule and Alan Meltzer's is that
   - a. McCallum's rule allows for the difference between current and desired GDP.
   - b. Meltzer's rule controls the federal-funds rate.
   - c. Meltzer's rule doesn't allow for changes in velocity.
   - d. McCallum's rule is based on real GDP, not nominal.
   - e. McCallum's rule focuses on nonborrowed reserves.

2. Monetarism was most popular
   - a. in the 1930s when declining money supply intensified the depression.
   - b. in the 1980s as velocity stabilized.
   - c. in the 1960s and 1970s as the Fed's inability to control inflation eroded their support.
   - d. in the 1990s as the movement for free markets and no government controls became stronger.
   - e. at the turn of the century when the gold standard was in vogue.

3. The Fed supports a law binding it to a low inflation goal because
   - a. that would shorten the lags in monetary policy.
   - b. that would avoid the time inconsistency problem. People would not expect the Fed to try to surprise them and therefore might be more willing to accept noninflationary wages and prices.
   - c. the Fed has learned it cannot trust itself.
   - d. Congress is forcing the Fed to be supportive.
   - e. full employment and exchange-rate stability just aren't important to the Fed.

4. The gold standard
   - a. implies that as the value of gold rises, say due to limited new supplies, prices of goods must fall, and this requires a recession.
   - b. guarantees no inflation.
   - c. is supported by most economists.
   - d. implies that money growth has an even more powerful effect on GDP because money would be worth more.
   - e. is supported by the U.S. Constitution.

5. Currency boards
   - a. are particularly subject to political pressure.
   - b. can follow discretionary policy.
   - c. fix the exchange rate between the local currency and some important foreign currency(ies).

    d.   imply that high inflation will create trade surplus.

    e.   sell local currency in periods of high inflation.

6.   Private money
   - *a.*   means people can print their own.
   - *b.*   could take the form of a contract to provide on demand *x* number of standard commodity bundles.
   - *c.*   still requires a Federal Reserve System.
   - *d.*   would still create a recession if people chose to hold more money.
   - *e.*   would still be a poor inflation hedge.

7.   A populist standard
   - *a.*   would control inflation through an incomes policy.
   - *b.*   would eliminate the Fed entirely.
   - *c.*   is supported by the majority of economists.
   - *d.*   is based on the belief that higher interest rates reduce inflation.
   - *e.*   advocates income inequality to spur work effort and savings.

8.   Monetarists
   - *a.*   want to increase Fed discretion.
   - *b.*   believe the Fed needs to pursue countercyclical policy more aggressively.
   - *c.*   fundamentally do not trust central banks.
   - *d.*   believe money has a direct and reliable connection to short-run variations in real GDP.
   - *e.*   rely on incomes policies to control inflation.

9.   The gold standard does not prevent the Fed from creating inflation if
   - *a.*   more gold is discovered.
   - *b.*   other countries also create inflation.
   - *c.*   full employment requires inflation.
   - *d.*   unions demand unreasonable wage increases.
   - *e.*   both *a* and *b*.

10.   Friedman claims that only part of the argument for a monetary growth rate rule is economic. The other part is
    - *a.*   religious.
    - *b.*   psychological.
    - *c.*   sociological.
    - *d.*   political
    - *e.*   scientific.

Topics for Discussion

1. Are currency boards a long-run solution? If not, what should countries in Eastern Europe and Russia be doing as the curency board acts as a stop gap?

2. It has been suggested that government should define money but not issue it. Government defines rulers, yard sticks, and miles but does not issue them. How would such a system work?

3. Recall how the gold standard failed. Are currency boards subject to the same problems?

Exercise Questions

1. Countries in Eastern Europe and Russia are often advised to adopt currency boards but are rarely advised to use a gold standard. Both force the central bank to fix the currency value, so why are currency boards favored?

2. The three feedback rules discussed in the text may be written as:

   Rule 1: $\Delta b_t = \Delta z_t - \Delta \bar{v} + \lambda(z^*_{t-1} - z_{t-1})$
   Rule 2: $\Delta b_t = \Delta z_t - \Delta \bar{v}$
   Rule 3: $\Delta b_t = 3 - \Delta \bar{v} + (z^*_{t-1} - z_{t-1})$

   where Δb is the change in the base, Δz the change in nominal GDP, $\Delta \bar{v}$ the change in velocity and λ a fraction between 0 and 1. All variables are four-year moving averages, and a * indicates a desired level.

   a. Which rule is advocated by McCallum? Meltzer? Judd?

   b. Which rule gives the Fed least discretion? Most discretion? Why?

   c. Which rule does not allow the Fed to increase base growth if there is a supply shock, such as an increase in oil prices?

   d. Which rule allows the Fed to alter policy to combat a recession of average duration?

Answers to Self-Tests

Completion

1.	monetary standard	4.	incomes
2.	rising, fall	5.	gold standard
3.	feedback rule	6.	currency board

CHAPTER 28 / 249

7.	economies of scale	9.	reduce
8.	increased	10.	nominal income

True-False

1.	False	6.	False
2.	True	7.	False
3.	False	8.	True
4.	True	9.	False
5.	True	10.	False

Multiple Choice

1.	*a*	6.	*b*
2.	*c*	7.	*a*
3.	*b*	8.	*c*
4.	*a*	9.	*e*
5.	*c*	10.	*d*

Answers to Exercise Questions

1. The value of a currency, like the dollar, yen, or deutschemark, is regulated by a central bank that has earned significant trust. There is no corresponding agency controlling the value of gold.

2. *a.* Rule 3; Rule 2; Rule 1.
   b. Rule 2; Rule 3; Rule 3 allows the Fed to state a desired nominal income growth rate.
   c. Rule 3. It is the only rule that doesn't allow current nominal income growth to affect base growth.
   d. None of the above. Recessions last about 9 months and the rules are based on 48-month moving averages. Note that the average cycle lasts about four years so that the rules are all roughly cycle independent.

CHAPTER 29   The Evolution of the
International Monetary System

Learning Objectives

1. Describe the three international monetary systems of the last century.

2. Cite the advantages and disadvantages of each system.

3. Discuss the factors that caused one system to give way in favor of the
    next one.

Key Terms, Concepts, and Institutions

gold standard
gold-exchange standard
Bretton Woods System
bimetallic standard
pegged exchange rates
limping gold standard
bills of exchange
International Bank for
    Reconstruction and Development
    (IBRD or World Bank)
post-Bretton Woods System
rules of the game
Bretton Woods institutions
mint parity
European Currency Unit (ECU)

International Trade
    Organization (ITO)
GATT (General Agreement on
    Tariffs and Trade)
International Monetary Fund
    (IMF)
SDRs (Special Drawing Rights)
floating exchange rate
Smithsonian Agreement
exchange rate
handling charges
General Arrangements to Borrow
gold flows
European Community (EC)

Self-Test: Completion

1. An alternative to shipping gold, which lowered shipping and insurance costs, was to ship _____ .

2. A country that shipped gold to settle a balance-of-payments deficit (increased/decreased) its money supply and (increased/decreased) its national price level.

3. The _____ standard developed as a result of an anticipated shortage of gold in the 1920s.

4. Under the gold-exchange standard, the two countries that did not have to ship gold in response to balance-of-payments deficits were

   _____ and _____ .

5. The _____ makes loans to countries to help them get through temporary foreign-exchange difficulties.

6. The _____ is a Bretton Woods institution which was created to facilitate the postwar reconstruction in Europe and which now extends financial assistance to developing countries.

7. The dominant agency promoting tariff reductions and the removal of other trade barriers is the _____ .

8. The IMF issues _____ , an international asset consisting of a market basket of the major currencies.

9. The _____ of 1972 resulted in the devaluation of the U.S. dollar.

10. The current international monetary system is _____ .

Self-Test: True-False

1. The gold standard came about as a result of international agreements.

2. Adherence to the gold standard resulted in pegged exchange rates.

3. Under the gold standard, gold would flow out of a country that incurred a balance-of-payments deficit.

4. Countries under the gold standard had complete control of their money supplies.

5. The advantage of the gold standard was the potential for stable commodity prices in the long run.

6. The IMF lends money to member countries without exacting any conditions from them as to how they intend to run their economic policies.

7. The value of special drawing rights is specified by the IMF in terms of gold.

8. The U.S. balance-of-payments deficits from 1950 to the mid-1960s resulted from a decline in the competitiveness of U.S. manufactured goods.

9. Countries on a limping gold standard increased the price of gold whenever the demand for gold increased.

10. A country whose imports exceed its exports has a balance-of-trade surplus.

Self-Test: Multiple Choice

1. U.S. balance-of-payments deficits from 1950 to the mid-1960s were primarily the result of
   a. the desire of other countries to add to their dollar holdings.
   b. an increase in petroleum imports.
   c. the loss of the competitive edge by U.S. manufacturers.
   d. a high U.S. inflation rate relative to the inflation rate of its major trading partners.
   e. all the above.

2. Today most of the major trading countries are on a
   a. gold-exchange standard.
   b. gold standard.
   c. limping gold standard.
   d. floating exchange-rate system.
   e. bimetallic system.

3. If the exchange rate of francs in terms of dollars is FF1 = $0.193, then the exchange rate of dollars in terms of francs is
   a. FF107.1.
   b. FF5.18.
   c. FF0.0093.
   d. $107.1.
   e. $5.18.

4. Under the gold standard, if the official price of gold increased, market forces would cause
   a. the money supply to increase and the price level to fall.

b.   the money stock to increase and the price level to rise.
c.   the money stock to decrease and the price level to fall.
d.   the money stock to decrease and the price level to rise.
e.   no change in the money supply or prices.

5.   Under the gold standard, exchange rates were
a.   fixed.
b.   flexible within narrow limits.
c.   fixed by central banks.
d.   completely flexible.
e.   none of the above.

6.   Under flexible exchange rates, an increase in U.S. imports of Japanese cars would cause
a.   the dollar to rise against the yen.
b.   the yen to rise against the dollar.
c.   gold to flow into the United States.
d.   gold to flow out of the United States.
e.   a and c.

7.   Under the rules of the game of the gold standard countries with balance-of-payments
a.   deficits would increase their money stocks.
b.   deficits would decrease their money stocks.
c.   surpluses would increase their money stocks.
d.   surpluses would decrease their money stocks.
e.   b and c.

8.   Under the gold standard, if the supply of gold increased rapidly due to new gold discoveries in South Africa, the
a.   general price level would rise for all countries on the gold standard.
b.   general price level would rise in South Africa.
c.   general price level would fall for all countries on the gold standard.
d.   general price level would fall in South Africa.
e.   price level would not change.

9.   A country experiencing balance-of-payments problems would apply for a loan to the
a.   World Bank.
b.   ITO.
c.   IMF.
d.   IBRD.
e.   a and c.

10. The Bretton Woods System
    a. established the IMF.
    b. established the World Bank.
    c. was the result of an international treaty.
    d. was established under the premise that there would be a perpetual dollar shortage.
    e. all the above.

Topics for Discussion

1. Some critics suggest that the United States could attain price stability if only it would return to the gold standard. What would have to be done for the United States to return to the gold standard? Would this guarantee stable prices?

2. Explain how the *expectation* of a devaluation could cause the devaluation to occur under fixed exchange rates.

3. It has been said that the Bretton Woods System creates a restrictive policy bias for countries with chronic balance-of-payments deficits. Explain how this could be true.

4. Compare and contrast the functions of the IBRD and the IMF.

5. Discuss the advantages and disadvantages of fixed versus flexible exchange rates.

Exercise Questions

1. The *Wall Street Journal* of September 13, 1983, reported that Zaire had decided to float its currency, the zaire. The zaire had been pegged to the IMF's special drawing rights since 1967. The zaire was devalued from a rate comparable to 6.06 per U.S. dollar to 29.9 per U.S. dollar.

    a. Bankers and diplomats praised Zaire's decision to devalue. What major group will benefit from this devaluation?

    b. The decision to devalue was a blow to black marketers in Zaire. Why? (What had they been doing?)

2. The following report is from the *Wall Street Journal*, September 13, 1983.

    Brazil has promised to sign by Thursday the letter of intent that is expected to release new credits from the International Monetary Fund. . . . Details of Brazil's letter of intent to the IMF weren't disclosed, but the document is supposed to lay out Brazil's promises through 1984 for curbing inflation and restoring more order to its financial house. . . .

    a.   Brazil applied to the IMF and not the World Bank. What does it need the loans for?

    b.   How does the IMF justify intervening in Brazil's internal affairs by requiring it to lay out proposals for curbing inflation, etc.?

3.   If the U.S. dollar will buy 151 Mexican pesos, how many dollars will a Mexican peso buy?

4.   Complete the table below.

System	Type of reserve asset	Mechanism for adjusting deficits/ surpluses
Gold standard		
Gold-exchange standard		
Bretton Woods		

5.   The ailing U.S. dollar hit a new post-Wold War II low against the yen. . . . Traders say the damage could have been worse, but fears of another international intervention made investors nervous about making big bets against the dollar . . . *Wall Street Journal,* April 7, 1995, p. C1.

    a.   The Bundesbank and the Bank of Japan had recently intervened to bolster the dollar. Why would they do that?

    b.   If the United States were under the gold standard, gold would (flow into/flow out of) the United States and the Fed would be forced to pursue (expansionary/contractionary) monetary policy.

6.   In January, 1995, some Republicans pushed for language requiring the Mexican government to accept a goal of restoring the Mexican peso to

its pre-devaluation exchange rate of 3.5 pesos to the dollar in exchange for $40 billion of U.S. loan guarantees. At the time, the exchange rate was 5.67 pesos to the dollar, and the value of the peso had been falling and seemed likely to continue to fall. *Wall Street Journal,* January 20, 1995, p. A3. Why did the Republicans push for the pre-devaluation exchange rate?

Answers to Self-Tests

Completion

1. bills of exchange
2. decreased; decreased
3. gold-exchange
4. Great Britain, the United States
5. International Monetary Fund (IMF)
6. International Bank for Reconstruction and Development (IBRD, or World Bank)
7. GATT (General Agreement on Tariffs and Trade)
8. SDRs (Special Drawing Rights)
9. Smithsonian Agreement
10. floating exchange rates

True-False

1.	False	6.	False
2.	True	7.	False
3.	True	8.	False
4.	False	9.	True
5.	True	10.	False

Multiple Choice

1.	a	6.	b
2.	d	7.	e
3.	b	8.	a
4.	b	9.	c
5.	b	10.	e

Answers to Exercise Questions

1. *a.* Exporters. Their goods will be cheaper now in terms of other countries.

    b. It wiped out the gap between the official and black market rates for the zaire, and the opportunity to profit by this differential.

2.   *a.* The fact that Brazil applied to the IMF and not to the World Bank indicates that the loans are to cover short-term balance-of-payments problems as opposed to long-term capital-financing projects.

    b. The IMF takes the view that credit should be extended only if there is a reasonable prospect that the member country can resolve its balance-of-payments problems.

3. $0.0066225 = 1 peso.

4.

System	Type of reserve asset	Mechanism for adjusting deficits/ surpluses
Gold standard	Gold	Changes in national money supplies
Gold-exchange standard	Gold, assets denominated in pounds or dollars	U.S. & Great Britain did not adjust their money supply; others did
Bretton Woods	SDRs, dollars, pounds	Currency devaluations or revaluations under IMF guidelines

5.   *a.* A weak dollar makes German and Japanese goods more expensive for their customers in the United States.

    b. flow out of, contractionary

6.   The weak peso made U.S. exports expensive in Mexico.

CHAPTER 30   Exchange Rates and the Balance of Payments

Learning Objectives

1. Understand the major forces behind supply of and demand for one currency versus supply of and demand for another.

2. Explain how institutions conduct the exchange of one currency for another.

3. Explain why the purchasing-power parity theory helps explain the changes in the relative values of currencies.

4. Show the interrelationships between the spot and forward rates between two currencies and the two countries' interest rates.

5. Understand how the expected spot rate and the forward rate for any currency are related.

6. Understand how importers and exporters can use the forward exchange markets to reduce risk.

7. Explain how and why central banks intervene in the foreign-exchange market.

8. Explain how the segmentation of national money markets affects a country's ability to use monetary policy to affect real variables.

9. Read the balance-of-payments accounts.

Key Terms, Concepts, and Institutions

exchange rate	speculators
balance of payments	arbitragers
fixed vs. floating exchange rates	purchasing-power parity theory
bid-ask spread	Fisher proposition

spot-exchange rate
payments balance
currency areas
swap contracts
balance-of-payments accounts
optimum currency-area issue
forward exchange rate
interest-rate parity theorem

intervention
forward premium
forward discount
spot transactions
forward transactions
trade balance
current account
capital account

Self-Test: Completion

1. If someone contracts today to trade marks for dollars at an agreed-on price in 30 days, they have sold marks _____ .

2. If someone agrees to deliver marks in two days at an agreed-on price, they have used the _____ market.

3. If a bank has more mark-denominated assets than liabilities, then it has taken a _____ position in marks.

4. If the inflation rate in the United States is lower than the rate in Germany, then the mark/dollar exchange rate will tend to _____ according to the _____ theorem.

5. If the interest rates in Germany increased, then the forward premium of the mark would tend to _____ according to the _____ theorem.

6. If people expect that the spot exchange rate will rise in the future, then the current spot exchange rate will tend to _____ .

7. Someone who uses her unusually low transactions costs to buy some currency where its price is low and sell it where its price is high, or uses the forward and spot exchange markets plus the capital markets to make an instantaneous riskless profit is a(n) _____ .

8. Someone who makes money by correctly guessing how spot or forward exchange rates will change is a(n) _____ .

9. If the U.S. stock market has a record boom, the foreign purchase of U.S. assets will tend to _____ the value of the dollar.

10. If foreign tourists buy U.S. goods by using traveler's checks drawn against their hometown bank, this would increase the _____ account, reduce the _____ account, and tend to _____ the value of the dollar.

11. Through the summer of 1986 the dollar was falling partly in response to rapid monetary growth here. Paul Volcker wanted other countries to help slow the dollar's slide. He asked them to _____ their interest rates.

Self-Test: True-False

1. Transactions costs for forward exchange rates are higher for more volatile currencies.

2. A U.S. importer of Japanese cars could get the yen he will need by selling yen forward.

3. Most exchanges between foreign currencies and the dollar occur within the United States.

4. If you know you will need marks in the future, you could buy marks now and invest in Germany, or you could invest in the United States and buy marks forward.

5. If you believe the spot mark/dollar rate will be 2 in 90 days, and the currently quoted 90-day future rate is 3, then you believe it would be profitable to sell marks forward and meet the contractual obligation by buying marks at the spot rate in 90 days.

6. Exchange rates have been more variable than the purchasing-power parity theory would seem to indicate.

7. Currencies are very nearly perfect substitutes for each other because there is little uncertainty in foreign-exchange markets.

8. It has been demonstrated that those who use the forward exchange markets to reduce risk pay a heavy risk premium.

9. If a currency is more expensive in the forward- than spot-exchange markets, then it is at a forward discount.

10. According to the purchasing-power parity theory, if the rate of inflation of tradeable goods is 5 percent higher in the United States than in Germany, then the mark/dollar rate should decline 5 percent a year.

Self-Test: Multiple Choice

1. If the forward premium on marks is larger than the difference between U.S. and German interest rates, then it would be more profitable to
   a. invest in the United States than in Germany.
   b. invest in Germany rather than the United States.
   c. borrow in Germany rather than the United States.
   d. sell marks forward and acquire the marks you will need in the spot-exchange market thirty days from now.
   e. buy marks forward and sell them in the spot-exchange market in thirty days.

2. If you know you will receive marks in the future and you want to insulate yourself from exchange-rate risk, you can
   a. sell dollars forward.
   b. buy marks forward.
   c. sell marks forward.
   d. sell marks spot.
   e. take out an insurance policy with the Chicago Mercantile Exchange.

3. If the mark/dollar rate is 2.6 and the yen/dollar rate is 243, then the yen/mark rate must be
   a. 631.8.
   b. .236.
   c. 48.6.
   d. .0107.
   e. 93.5.

4. The bid-ask spread
   a. is larger in big city banks than in smaller banks.
   b. first states the exchange rate used when buying marks from customers and then states the exchange rate used when providing customers with marks.
   c. is set by a cartel.
   d. tends to be larger for more stable currencies.
   e. is at least equal to 1 percent of the dollar value of the transaction.

5. The forward exchange rate is likely to be an unbiased predictor of the future spot exchange rate because
   a. the willingness of each group of importers to pay a risk premium tends to be offsetting.
   b. it is estimated by skilled economists.
   c. on average the actual mark/dollar spot exchange rate is below the rate predicted by the forward exchange market.

    d. the uncertainty of foreign exchange demands a risk premium.

    e. exchange rates are stable enough so that it is easy to make accurate predictions.

6. The purchasing-power parity theory
   a. is a theory of social justice.
   b. states that tradable goods in different countries should have the same price after an allowance is made for transportation costs and the exchange rate.
   c. is a relationship between the forward premium or discount and interest rates.
   d. depends critically on what people expect the spot exchange rate will be in the future.
   e. quite accurately predicts short-term movements in exchange rates.

7. The Fisher proposition
   a. depends on arbitragers.
   b. is a relationship linking the inflation rates of two countries.
   c. depends on speculators to bet on their guesses about the future spot exchange rates of some currency.
   d. states that if the interest rate in the United States is higher than the interest rate in Germany, then speculators believe the mark/dollar rate will increase.
   e. is identical to the interest-rate parity theorem.

8. A central bank could intervene in the foreign-exchange markets
   a. to keep its currency from appreciating by buying its own currency with foreign-exchange reserves.
   b. to keep its currency from depreciating by selling its own currency and building up foreign-exchange reserves.
   c. to encourage currency appreciation by reducing the domestic money stock, which leads to a higher interest rate.
   d. to encourage currency depreciation by reducing inflation.
   e. to encourage exports by buying its own currency.

9. Central bank intervention
   a. is currently required of the United States to maintain a stated dollar/gold exchange rate.
   b. is much less frequent than it used to be under the Bretton Woods System.
   c. depends on the size of foreign-exchange reserves that central banks have or are willing to maintain.
   d. rarely conflicts with domestic monetary policy.
   e. always changes the domestic money supply.

10. Domestic monetary policy is likely to have larger domestic and smaller foreign effects if
    a. exchange rates are fixed.
    b. currencies are good substitutes for each other.
    c. tariff barriers are removed.
    d. exchange rates fluctuate unpredictably.
    e. all but d.

Topics for Discussion

1. What are the major advantages of a fixed exchange-rate system?

2. What are the major advantages of a flexible exchange-rate system?

3. Does the presence of a forward exchange market for periods up to a year mean importers and exporters face no foreign-exchange-rate risk?

4. Why is the Fisher proposition likely to be a better guide when exchange rates are relatively stable?

5. Purchasing-power parity depends on trade of physical goods. What sort of price index would fit the theory best?

6. Is purchasing-power parity likely to be a better predictor of exchange rates in the short run or the long run? Why?

7. On October 1, 1986, the *Wall Street Journal* reported that the West German central bank was buying dollars. Volcker continued his plea for lower German interest rates to achieve the same end. What difference does it make whether the German central bank boosts the dollar by direct purchases or by reducing its interest rates?

8. The *Wall Street Journal* article titled "U.S. Treasury Debt Is Increasingly Traded Globally and Nonstop" (September 10, 1986, p. 1) reported that the international trading of U.S. government debt has been spurred by the huge U.S. deficit, deregulation of financial markets abroad, U.S. regulations allowing foreign markets abroad, and U.S. regulations allowing foreign investors to buy government securities tax free.

   Why do we give foreign investors a tax break? How does this affect the dollar value? Our exports? Which industries and governments benefit from the flow of capital from abroad to the United States? Which lose?

Exercise Questions

1. Calculate the price in pounds of a Chevette selling for $10,000 given the following exchange rates:

   Pounds/dollar = .75   pound price (*a:* _____)

   Pounds/dollar = 1.0   pound price (*b:* _____)

   Given these calculations, we expect the quantity of Chevettes sold in Britain to (*c:* increase/decrease) as the pound price of the dollar rises. This helps explain why the (*d:* demand for/supply of) dollars is (*e:* upward/downward) sloping.

   Calculate the price in dollars of an M.G.B. midget whose pound sterling price is 7,500 given the exchange rates below:

   Pounds/dollar = .75   dollar price (*f:* _____)

   Pounds/dollar = 1.0   dollar price (*g:* _____)

   Given these calculations, we expect the quantity of midgets sold in the United States to (*h:* increase/decrease) as the pound price of the dollar rises. This helps explain why the (*i:* demand for/supply of) dollars is (*j:* upward/downward) sloping.

2. An increase in U.S. interest rates will (*a:* increase/decrease) the demand for dollars as more people with pounds choose to buy U.S. rather than U.K. securities. Similarly, the higher U.S. interest rates will (*b:* increase/decrease) the supply of dollars as more people with dollars choose to buy U.S. securities. These two effects lead to a (*c:* higher/lower) pound/dollar exchange rate. This is a(n) (*d:* appreciation/depreciation) of the dollar.

   An increase in the U.S. rate of inflation would (*e:* increase/decrease) the supply of dollars as people with dollars try to buy more U.K. goods and would (*f:* increase/decrease) the demand for dollars as people with pounds buy fewer U.S. goods. These two effects lead to a (*g:* higher/lower) pound/dollar exchange rate. This is a(n) (*h:* appreciation/depreciation) of the dollar.

3. The following data are taken from the June 5, 1995, issue of the *Wall Street Journal*:

Marks/dollar spot exchange rate	1.4085
Marks/dollar 180-day forward exchange rate	1.4023
U.S. prime interest rate	9%
German prime interest rate	4.5%

The dollar is selling at an annual forward *a:* _____ against the mark of *b:* _____ percent. Apparently, markets believe the dollar will *c:* appreciate/depreciate) against the mark. The difference in expected currency values (*d:* is/is not) equal to the difference in interest rates. (The fact that interest parity is not doing a particularly good job of predicting spot and forward rates has led some observers to claim the market is not driven by fundamentals. Many forecasters have returned to an earlier methodology that places heavier emphasis on the trade balance.)

Answers to Self-Tests

Completion

1. forward
2. spot
3. long
4. rise, purchasing-power parity
5. decline, interest-rate parity
6. rise
7. arbitrager
8. speculator
9. increase
10. current, capital, increase
11. lower

True-False

1. True
2. False
3. False
4. True
5. False
6. True
7. False
8. False
9. False
10. True

Multiple Choice

1. b
2. c
3. e
4. b
5. a
6. b
7. c
8. c
9. c
10. d

Answers to Exercise Questions

1. a. 7,500
    b. 10,000
    c. decrease
    d. demand for
    e. downward
    f. 10,000
    g. 7,500
    h. increase
    i. supply of
    j. upward

2.
   - *a.* increase
   - *b.* decrease
   - *c.* higher
   - *d.* appreciation
   - *e.* increase
   - *f.* decrease
   - *g.* lower
   - *h.* depreciation

3.
   - *a.* discount
   - *b.* 0.9
   - *c.* depreciate
   - *d.* is not

CHAPTER 31   Future Directions for the International Monetary System

Learning Objectives

1. Explain why regions with a single labor market and capital mobility may find it to their advantage to have a single currency.

2. Show why independent monetary policy requires exchange-rate uncertainty and money-market segmentation.

3. Outline the arguments of those who favor pegged exchange rates.

4. Outline the arguments of those who favor floating exchange rates.

5. List the relative merits of gold and the dollar as the international reserve asset.

6. Explain why a new international economic order will be difficult to establish.

Key Terms, Concepts, and Institutions

international monetary system
monetary independence
pegged exchange rates
optimal currency area
labor market
segmented markets
political unification

ECU
floating exchange rates
crawling peg exchange system
passive borrowing
seigniorage
European Monetary System
reserve assets

Self-Test: Completion

1. The motives for currency unification in Europe include political
   _____ , the growth of _____ , and creation of a large
   center of _____ stability.

2. Under the Bretton Woods System, international reserve assets could be
   increased only if the United States ran a payments _____ . The
   problem was that such deficits meant the gold backing of dollars
   _____ .

3. If it is possible to have different interest rates on similar securities in
   two different countries, then the capital markets are said to be
   _____ .

4. It is sometimes argued that the speculative sale of a currency can lead to
   its devaluation, which in turn will generate inflation since imports will
   be more expensive. The inflation justifies the currency
   devaluation. This is an example of _____ speculation.

5. If countries routinely adjust the pegged exchange rates several times a
   year, the scheme is called a _____ peg.

6. The European Community has developed a new currency called the
   _____ that may eventually compete with the dollar as an
   international reserve asset.

7. More expansive monetary policy would tend to lower interest rates and
   increase expected inflation. Both effects cause the currency to
   _____ .

8. As long as foreign governments were willing to hold more dollars as
   reserves, the United States was able to finance payments deficits through
   _____ .

9. By being the international banker, the United States earns a profit from
   the production of money called _____ .

10. One of the major advantages of an institution creating international
    reserves is that reserves could be _____ .

Self-Test: True-False

1. Any new international financial arrangements would have to be consistent with the distribution of political and economic power.

2. The Bretton Woods System broke down in 1971 because of an undervalued dollar and because the inflation rates in other countries were too high.

3. Critics of flexible rates argue that increased monetary freedom will lead to greater inflation.

4. An advantage of the crawling-peg system over a fixed-rate system is that it would reduce speculation on exchange-rate changes.

5. Currency unification will be less costly if the capital market for the region is segmented.

6. If changes in monetary policy lead to rapid fluctuations in expected inflation, then the spot-exchange rate will fluctuate rapidly even if the inflation rate is fairly stable.

7. As a practical matter, the best time to switch to a system of fixed exchange rates is whenever the differences between inflation rates of trading partners are large.

8. The floating rate system has generated more stable exchange rates than had been anticipated.

9. One of the arguments for a fixed exchange-rate system is that it leads to more segmented capital markets and increases the independence of monetary policy.

10. The fact that the dollar is an international reserve asset may constrain monetary policy. The Fed may be anxious to maintain foreign demand for the dollar, and this may limit the variations in interest rates and exchange rates it believes it can allow.

Self-Test: Multiple Choice

1. Currency unification is more likely to be beneficial if
    a. labor markets are segmented.
    b. the merging countries are already quite large.
    c. the business cycles in the countries are similar in timing and amplitude.
    d. before unification different interest rates on similar securities were common.
    e. the countries each have their own language.

2. New international financial arrangements
   a. may have virtually no cost if the treaties merely describe present practices.
   b. are less likely to involve a strong central authority if nationalist pressures become stronger.
   c. would have to give special status to the United States, Europe, and Japan to be viable.
   d. could offer a forum to coordinate national economic policies.
   e. all the above.

3. The interwar experience with floating exchange rates led to the belief that
   a. speculation tends to be stabilizing.
   b. floating rates disrupt trade and investment.
   c. floating rates reduce monetary independence.
   d. the interwar inflation was caused by floating rates.
   e. none of the above.

4. The uncertainty of floating exchange rates
   a. disrupts trade but differentiates national currencies and allows for independent monetary policy.
   b. disrupts trade and has no offsetting benefits.
   c. can be perfectly hedged through the use of forward exchange contracts and therefore imposes no costs.
   d. has a greater impact on large, self-sufficient economies.
   e. means the forward exchange rate will be a biased predictor of the future spot exchange rate.

5. One of the problems of managing a pegged-rate system is
   a. changes in parity tend to occur before they are needed.
   b. countries must be willing to pay the domestic political cost of keeping the inflation rates in different countries close to each other.
   c. no one pays much attention when parities are changed.
   d. providing reserves to countries with payments deficits.
   e. b and d.

6. Reserve assets
   a. declined alarmingly in the 1970s.
   b. consist entirely of gold.
   c. could only be created in the 1960s if the United States ran payments deficits.
   d. probably helped reduce world inflation in the 1970s.
   e. have been kept on a stable growth path by the IMF.

7. The use of the dollar as a reserve asset
    a. has increased despite the demise of the Bretton Woods System.
    b. exposes the United States to risk, since these dollars could be dumped in exchange for another currency.
    c. is due to the extensive trade and financial links the United States has with the rest of the world.
    d. would decline if foreigners lost faith in the ability or resolve of the Fed to control inflation.
    e. all the above.

8. A return to a system of fixed exchange rates would be aided most by
    a. rising nationalism.
    b. a wide range of emerging economic powers.
    c. segmented labor markets.
    d. similar rates of inflation among the large trading partners.
    e. the invention of a manageable reserve asset.

9. Stop-go monetary policies are likely to lead to
    a. more variable exchange rates than the purchasing-power parity theory would suggest because the spot price is affected by both the present and expected future values of a currency.
    b. less variable exchange rates than the purchasing-power parity theory would suggest.
    c. more variable exchange rates because if people suddenly expect more inflation in the United States, they will acquire dollars before prices rise.
    d. more variable exchange rates because a lower interest rate would lead people to acquire more dollars.
    e. a return to a fixed exchange-rate system.

Topics for Discussion

1. Would the United States and Mexico be good candidates for currency unification? How about England and Germany?

2. Do you think fixed exchange rates would help reduce inflation or would countries simply abandon fixed rates whenever internal and external goals came into conflict?

3. Robert Mundell of Columbia University believes the argument for flexible exchange rates is severely weakened by the fact that currency regions are political rather than economic. His argument begins with a hypothetical situation. Suppose the United States and Canada are discussing whether to peg exchange rates. In the eastern half of both countries there is inflation associated with the rapid growth in

automobile production. In the western half of both countries there is a recession due to the slow-moving forest products industry. Consider why Mundell would conclude that the case for flexible rates is logically strong only if currencies are regional rather than national.[1]

4. Is the current account likely to be in surplus or deficit for less-developed countries? Is this because they are borrowing in order to grow or because they cannot produce enough goods and services?

5. What are the disadvantages of gold as a reserve asset? The dollar?

6. Why do flexible exchange rates lead to segmented capital markets?

Exercise Questions

1. Purchasing-power parity requires that the price level in the United States equal the price level in Great Britain once the difference in exchange rates is accounted for. The relative form of the purchasing-power parity theory states that the inflation rate in the United States plus the percentage appreciation of the dollar will equal the inflation rate in Britain. This relationship works reasonably well in the long run but not the short run.

    In the long run, then, if the inflation rate in the United States is 10 percent and the inflation rate in Britain is 7 percent, we would expect

    (*a:* an appreciation/adepreciation) of the dollar of (*b:*_____) percent. This means dollars should sell at a forward (*c:* premium/discount) of

    (*d:*_____) percent.

    Under a fixed exchange-rate system, the pound price of the dollar would (*e:* appreciate/depreciate/not change). In order to maintain this exchange rate, the inflation rate in the United States must be (*f:* greater than/equal to/less than) the inflation rate in Britain. This implies that the monetary policies of both countries (*g:* are independent/must be coordinated).

    Under a fixed exchange-rate system, then the dollar would sell at a

    forward (*h:* premium/discount/neither) of (*i:*_____) percent. Given the interest-rate parity theorem, the interest rate in the United States would be (*j:* greater than/less than/equal to) the interest rate in the United Kingdom. Any attempt by the Fed to increase the interest rate would (*k:* succeed/ fail), since money would flow from (*l:* the United States to the United Kingdom/the United Kingdom to the United States).

[1]Mundell's argument is set out in his book, *International Economics* (New York: Macmillan Co., 1968), pp. 179–81.

Therefore, fixed rates (*m:* increase/reduce) capital mobility and (*n:* increase/reduce) the effectiveness of monetary policy.

2. During the last few years of the Bretton Woods System, the inflation rate in the United States was (*a:* higher/lower) than in Germany and Japan. This led to (*b:* more/fewer) U.S. exports and (*c:* more/fewer) U.S. imports. This meant that the dollar reserves held by Germany and Japan (*d:* rose/fell). At the end of the Bretton Woods System the dollar (*e:* appreciated/depreciated) and the value of these dollar holdings (*f:* increased/decreased). To the surprise of many, foreign official holdings of dollars (*g:* increased/decreased). This may have been done to reduce the (*h:* appreciation/depreciation) of the foreign currencies. Such an exchange-rate change would have meant that the foreign-goods cost (*i:* more/less) in terms of the dollar and U.S.-goods cost (*j:* more/less) in terms of their currency. Therefore they would have exported (*k:* more/less) and imported (*l:* more/less), and this would have led to (*m:* more/less) employment in their own country.

3. The peso tumbled nearly 10% in morning trading yesterday. . . . Finance Minister Guillermo Ortiz had hoped to win investors back by showing that Mexico would honor its debt payments and keep its currency convertible into dollars. Instead, the lack of investor confidence is feeding on itself. The crisis of confidence slams the peso, that creates more doubts, and that hammers the peso even more . . . *Wall Street Journal,* March 7, 1995, p. A3.

Opponents of floating exchange rates had predicted just such a scenario. If the international community returned to the gold standard, what would Mexico be forced to do?

4. In February 1995, Federal Reserve Governor Alan Greenspan said that he favored ". . . a return to the gold standard, though he allowed that he is probably the only Fed policymaker who does . . ." *Wall Street Journal,* March 7, 1995, p. A2.

Why do other Fed policy makers oppose a return to the gold standard? Why does Greenspan favor it?

Answers to Self-Tests

Completion

1. unification, trade, monetary
2. deficit; declined
3. segmented
4. destabilizing
5. crawling
6. ECU
7. depreciate
8. passive borrowing
9. seigniorage
10. managed

True-False

1. True
2. False
3. True
4. True
5. False

6. True
7. False
8. False
9. False
10. True

Multiple Choice

1. c
2. e
3. b
4. a
5. e

6. c
7. e
8. d
9. a

Answers to Exercise Questions

1.
   a. depreciation
   b. 3
   c. discount
   d. 3
   e. not change
   f. equal to
   g. must be coordinated
   h. neither

   i. 0
   j. equal to
   k. fail
   l. the United Kingdom to the United States
   m. increase
   n. reduce

2.
   a. higher
   b. fewer
   c. more
   d. rose
   e. depreciated
   f. decreased
   g. increased

   h. appreciation
   i. more
   j. less
   k. less
   l. more
   m. less

3. Under the gold standard, Mexico would be forced to ship gold; this would decrease the money supply. A restrictive monetary policy would increase interest rates; this would strengthen the peso.

4. The other Fed policy makers probably fear that it would be more difficult to pursue an independent monetary policy under the gold standard. Greenspan probably favors it because he favors policies to control inflation.